D0258291

In memory of

R. O. MORRIS

with gratitude

CONTENTS

ACKNOWLEDGEMENTS

Thanks are due to the following publishers for permission to quote illustrations from works in their catalogues:

Messrs. Edwin Ashdown Ltd.	R. Vaughan Williams: Silent Noon.
Messrs. Boosey & Co. Ltd.	R. Vaughan Williams: 'Clun' from On Wenlock Edge.
Messrs. Boosey & Hawkes Ltd.	Béla Bartók: Sixth String Quartet. N. Rimsky-Korsakov: Scheherazade. C. V. Stanford: Fairy Lough.
Messrs. Breitkopf & Haertel.	J. Sibelius: Second Symphony. 'The Bard.'
Messrs. J. B. Cramer & Co. Ltd.	C. V. Stanford: The Monkey's Carol.
Messrs. J. Curwen & Sons Ltd.	R. Vaughan Williams: Mass (Gloria). Psalm 90.
Messieurs Durand et Cie.	C. A. Debussy: La Demoiselle Élue. Quartet. M. Ravel: Quartet. Sonatine (Menuet). String Quartet.
Maison J. Hamelle.	G. Fauré: Requiem.
Messrs. Alfred Lengnick & Co. Ltd.	A. Dvořák: Second Symphony. Cello Concerto. 'New World' Symphony.
Messrs. Novello & Co. Ltd.	E. Grieg: Piano Concerto. Peer Gynt. A. Dvořák: Fourth Symphony. E. Elgar: The Kingdom. The Dream of Gerontius. Enigma Variations. H. Wolf: Italian Serenade. Grenzen der Menscheit. Rattenfänger. The Gardener (Mörike-lieder).
Messrs. Stainer & Bell, Ltd.	R. Vaughan Williams: Sea Symphony.

INTRODUCTION TO VOLUME TWO

This book is largely in the form of lecture notes, and is the direct outcome of teaching and lecturing at Oxford. It is intended to follow Dr. R. O. Morris's *The Oxford Harmony*, Vol. I, and deals with Chromatic Harmony and Modulation, and practical matters such as writing for string ensembles, pianoforte accompaniment, setting words to music, etc.

The point of view from which the subject is considered must be made clear at the outset. The study of musical theory is primarily regarded as a means of acquiring the elements of the technique of composition. Undoubtedly the best way of gaining the necessary knowledge would be for each student to make a detailed and critical study of all standard works from, say, 1500 to 1900, and from this to evolve a set of working rules to guide his practical efforts. It is said that J. S. Bach himself learnt his technique by this method. To-day the time factor and the enormous bulk of the corpus of standard works make it almost impossible for the student, however diligent, to do more than touch the fringes of the literature of his art; much less can he hope to examine it in detail from a highly critical technical standpoint. The work of the theorist should therefore be to provide him with an outline of the essential technique of composition according to the practice of composers whose work has stood the test of time. Such an outline must of necessity involve the exposition of a certain amount of ready-made theoretical hypotheses as a starting-point, as well as some arbitrary and dogmatic rules.

These theoretical rules must be thought of as deductions from the practice of accepted composers for the guidance of the student, and not as fundamental laws (in the Hobbesian sense) which composers were bound to follow. Viewed thus the grammar and syntax of music become as much a natural part of a living mode of expression as they are of any language. The student of Latin, for example, has to learn and obey rules of grammar and syntax deduced from the usage of great writers in that language; when he has mastered the language the rules become a subconscious part of his mastery of a medium of expression, just as they were a natural part of the language of Cicero. This parallel must not be pushed too far, but one more similarity may be pointed out; the grammar of a language changes in minor details from age to age; the same phenomenon is apparent in the historical study of the technique of musical composition; yet in both the basic principles remain constant.

In this book the main object has been to examine the use of certain important technical processes by composers of different periods, and follow the changes in their use, where such changes are important, through the period from about 1600 to 1900. For the sake of clarity and organization it has been found necessary to adopt the usual conventional conceptions of the theory of harmony as a starting-point and it is assumed that the reader has some knowledge of these.

The 'Fundamental Bass' theory which sought to explain harmony by acoustics is a thing of the past; it has been completely discredited on the acoustical side, and from the musical point of view it simply does not work. Some of the terminology bound up with it has passed into such common use that its retention, with very much altered significance, is probably necessary mainly for lack of better technical terms. The word 'root' is an important case in point. In the present book the term 'a chord with dominant (or tonic or supertonic, etc.) root' (or 'Dominant Harmony' for short) is simply used to signify that the chord under discussion is inherently dominant (or tonic, etc.) in its relationship to the key, the 'root' being no more than the bass note of the uninverted chord, which gives it its name. No idea of the root as a 'generator' is implied.

All diatonic triads, except that on the leading note which is in effect dominant harmony, are treated as individual harmonies each having a definite and characteristic relationship to the key in being at the time. The inversion of these chords does not alter their character in this relationship, nor in most cases does the addition of a seventh or ninth; they remain dominant (or tonic, etc) harmonies. A word must be said about the 'added sixth' chord, (Key C). Following the principle just stated this chord is treated as a first inversion of supertonic harmony with a (minor) seventh added. It must be admitted that this identification of this combination of notes (in the key of C) is open to question. To some musicians the effect might be that of a subdominant rather than a supertonic relationship. To the present writer the effect is almost always strongly supertonic. In any case it is not a matter of vital importance but rather one of classification.

Having discarded the Fundamental Bass theory of the origin of harmony, how then is the phenomenon to be explained? The hypothesis put forward is simply that harmony grew quite naturally out of counterpoint. It will be seen that in chromatic harmony almost every 'new' chord had its origin in some contrapuntal process, such as a chromatic passing note or appoggiatura, and eventually gained acceptance in its own right.

In approaching the study of harmony it is essential to realize from the start that the most important factor is the relationship of one chord to another and of those chords to a definite key. The notes C E G sounded together have practically no musical significance unless they are preceded or followed by some other combination of notes, and this progression in turn does not attain its full musical effect until it can be related to some key centre. In this matter of chord and key relationships certain basic principles seem to emerge such as root relationships and common notes. These connecting links have no scientific explanation, but are of great interest for the light which they throw on the way man's musical intelligence works.

Chapters XIII to XIX of the book deal with the application of theoretical knowledge to the actual writing of music. Of necessity examination requirements have had to be kept in view to a considerable extent, but in some universities examination questions are no longer either merely pedantic or completely unmusical; they are sometimes even excellent and musicianly preliminary exercises in composition. As far as possible the method adopted in this part of the book is the same as in the earlier part; an attempt to show how composers in the past dealt with the various problems which confront the student.

The technique of musical composition is only the means by which the composer can deliver his message; it is the quality of what he has to say that really matters. Nevertheless, whatever he has to say, it is his first duty to express himself clearly and cleanly, and for this purpose his technical equipment must be adequate. It is sheer folly to disregard the technique evolved by composers of the past, and it is only by serious study of their art that the musician of to-day can hope to find a sure foundation for his musical language.

Acknowledgements must be made to many of my friends and pupils who have given me much help and sound criticism in writing the book; chief among these the late Dr. R. O. Morris who first suggested that I should undertake the task, Mr. P. Platt of Magdalen College whose 'flair' for providing exactly the right example to illustrate some point has saved me many hours of search, and Mr. D. Cantrell of Keble College who has read the proofs with great care.

Chapter One

THE SUPERTONIC CHROMATIC CHORDS

A CHROMATIC chord may be defined as a chord containing one or more notes foreign to the prevailing key (i.e. diatonic scale).

Such chords may be used within the scope of the prevailing key without either implied or actual modulation. They may equally well be used as pivot chords for purposes of modulation. This will be discussed in the section dealing with modulation.

In this section it is the use of chromatic chords as strictly chromatic harmony, that is, without actual or implied modulation, that will be considered.

It is proposed to give some account of the chief chromatic chords in use during the period on which the study of harmony is usually based, (from the end of the sixteenth century to the early part of the twentieth), and examine instances of them in actual composition.

Chromatic harmony in the strict sense can be extremely effective. In Chapter IX an attempt is made to show some of the possibilities it opens up. For the moment it is enough to advise the student to use it very sparingly and only for some really good reason. It is an edged tool, and its effectiveness generally varies inversely with the frequency of its employment.

The supertonic chromatic chords generally recognized are:

(1) *The major common chord on the Supertonic* (i.e. the dominant chord of the dominant key), and its first inversion, which is even more common and generally more pleasant. (The second inversion is rarely found.)

(2) *The Supertonic Chromatic Seventh;* a minor seventh added to the supertonic chromatic common chord. The result is the dominant seventh of the dominant key. All the inversions are possible. Sometimes the root is left out.

(3) *The Supertonic Chromatic Ninth;* a ninth, major or minor in the major keys, minor only in the minor keys, may be added to the supertonic

chromatic common chord or seventh, either as an appoggiatura or as an essential note. In its inversions the chord usually sheds its root and in the case of the minor ninth becomes really a diminished seventh.

(4) *The Supertonic Chromatic Eleventh and Thirteenth.* It used to be customary to include these so-called 'higher supertonic discords' in the list of supertonic chromatic chords. The result of the addition of an eleventh or thirteenth is either merely an appoggiatura or a chord from which so many notes have to be omitted that it loses its supertonic identity. For example the following modest diatonic seventh has been theoretically described as a supertonic chromatic eleventh with the root and (major) third omitted, resolving on a dominant discord!

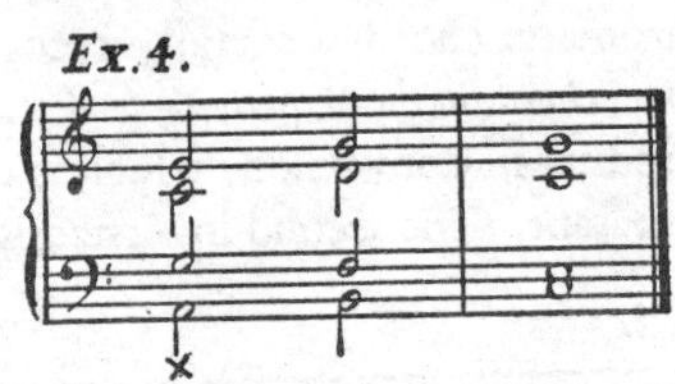

All these chords can be used in theory without modulation. The text-book rules for this are quite simple.

(1) The chord which precedes the supertonic chromatic chord should not be one which contains the (diatonic) fourth degree of the scale. (This is not born out by classical examples, see examples 8, 11b.)

(2) The chord of resolution should be either a dominant *discord*,[1] or some position of tonic harmony.

1 Theorists have probably gone too far in stressing the need for cancelling the effect of the sharpened fourth degree of the scale by using the dominant seventh when the chord resolves on dominant harmony in order to avoid modulation. Unless the cadence produced by the resolution on the plain dominant chord is emphasized there is really little or no feeling of modulation. The stock-in-trade resolution on the dominant seventh is often very weak.

(3) The major third of the chord should either rise or fall a semitone.

(4) The seventh behaves like any self-respecting diatonic seventh and falls by step or remains to form part of the new chord, or in certain cases rises by step. When the root is present the seventh should not be doubled.

(5) Ninths whether major or minor may be treated as appoggiaturas resolving by step within the chord, or may be regarded as essential notes and treated in the normal way.

The chord has had a chequered history. Its beginnings can be traced to the sixteenth century, where the following beautifully clean and moving progression, though it may arise from completely different conceptions, is often found.

By the time of Bach the chord was well established and in common use. It is found as part of the general harmonic vocabulary throughout the classical and romantic period, used frequently for purposes of modulation and as a purely chromatic chord. During the nineteenth century it became involved in the fashion for cloying chromaticism, and a possibly unwarranted reaction against it has grown up in the minds of musicians to-day.

Bach used the chord quite freely, especially as an approach to a cadence. It nearly always appears in an inverted form, and with a seventh or ninth added. Some examples given below will show his typical way of dealing with it.

These two examples show a perfectly normal use of the chord in its first inversion with the seventh added, approached in the first case from the submediant and resolved on a dominant discord, and in the second from a tonic $\frac{6}{4}$ and resolved on a plain dominant chord without any suggestion of modulation.

In these two examples the chord is approached from the tonic in root position and resolved on dominant harmony, perhaps the most common method. The first is an example of a supertonic minor ninth in the major key; the second a supertonic seventh in the minor key, both in the first inversion.

These examples show an approach from the supertonic and subdominant (see textbook rule I), and resolution on simple dominant harmony. This is so common and so musical as to suggest that the rule should be regarded merely as cautionary. In the first case the plain supertonic chromatic triad without seventh or ninth is shown, a rare occurrence in Bach. The second is a good example of an appoggiatura minor ninth.

The three examples above illustrate less common uses of the chord. The first is very striking, the supertonic chromatic seventh changing into a diatonic supertonic seventh before resolving on a dominant seventh. The second is merely a text-book resolution on a last inversion of a dominant seventh, but it seems to be uncommon in Bach. The third is a rare but interesting approach to the chord from a last inversion of a dominant seventh.

Two more examples from Bach must suffice to show both the resolution of the chord on tonic harmony and the chord itself in positions other than the first inversion. In the first case a root position supertonic chromatic seventh resolves on a tonic first inversion. In the second case, a first followed by a second inversion of the chromatic chord (plus an appoggiatura ninth) resolves on a tonic second inversion.

Handel, on the whole, used chromatic harmony much less freely than Bach. As might be expected, the supertonic chromatic chords are comparatively rarely found in his works as real chromatic chords, though they often appear in modulation. The first inversion, and the resulting diminished seventh are the forms most often seen. The following examples show much the same normal procedure as is found in Bach, but the chord seems to occur in Handel further away from the cadence, and its use is more regular and less enterprising, even if, possibly, because of its sporadic appearance, it is sometimes more striking.

In the Mozart–Haydn period the chord in root position becomes frequent. The following examples show the perfectly normal textbook use of the chord. The first inversion is of course also commonly found.

Beethoven uses the chord freely in the normal ways of his predecessors. In his later works it often seems to acquire a new emotional significance. The following examples will show something of this:

Schubert makes much use of these chords. The following examples show (a) the chord plus the seventh between two statements of the tonic chord over a pedal, and (b) the chord with an appoggiatura major ninth resolving on dominant harmony, also over a tonic pedal. The first is important; the supertonic chromatic chord is here an essential part of the melody.

There are many fine examples of these chords in the work of the Romantic composers, generally following the lines of classical usage. It must be admitted, however, that there is some inherent weakness and even sentimental tendency in their chromatic use, especially when the resolution is on a dominant discord. In the hands of second and third rate composers in an age when facile sentimentality was fashionable the chord became an easy vehicle for this form of expression. Even in the work of a composer of the stature of Mendelssohn this may be seen.

Of the less felicitous appearances of the chords little need be said. Perhaps one example will suffice. The fact that, save for the difference of mode, the progression is identical with that in the last Beethoven example will show that it is the context and musical intention behind the use of any chord rather than the chord itself or its method of resolution which ultimately makes good or bad music.

Brahms brought fresh significance to the chord. Very striking examples of its employment, often over a pedal, can be found throughout his work. In the first and third examples below he develops the use of the chord between two statements of tonic harmony already seen in Schubert. The second example shows an essential major ninth resolving on dominant harmony.

An example from Wolf's *Italian Serenade* shows a normal supertonic chromatic seventh with some delightful chromatic decorations.

To sum up: the most frequent use of these chords in the Bach–Handel period is in the first inversion, the seventh generally being present, resolution being upon dominant harmony or a $\begin{smallmatrix}6 & 5\\4 & 3\end{smallmatrix}$ on the dominant. The chord is aqually common in the major and minor modes. From the time of

Haydn the root position also comes into general use, and soon afterwards the resolution directly on to the tonic chord, which was so beautifully hinted at in the sixteenth century, again comes into favour. This is one of the cleanest and most telling resolutions, and was considerably developed by Brahms. The inherent tendency of the chord towards sentimentality became obvious in the weaker moments of the nineteenth century.

It should be borne in mind that the supertonic chromatic chord is really a variant of diatonic supertonic harmony. It will be seen later that it combines well with other variants of supertonic harmony.

Apart from its very great possibilities in modulation, it must be recognized that this chord has played a distinguished part in great music as a strictly chromatic chord, and it is only a sign of ignorance to dismiss it lightly as sentimental chromaticism long since outmoded. Two splendid modern examples are quoted to drive home this point. More will be said of them in a later chapter.

Chapter Two

THE MAJOR CHORD ON THE FLATTENED SUPERTONIC

THE major common chord on the flattened supertonic is one of the most important and beautiful things in Classical chromatic harmony.

In its first inversion the chord is commonly known as the *Neapolitan Sixth*, traditionally supposed to have been 'invented' by Alessandro Scarlatti and his followers. Whatever its origin it is a beautiful and expressive chord, which can be used either as strictly chromatic harmony, or in modulation with splendid effect.

Its normal resolution without modulation is upon some form of one of the primary triads, most commonly the dominant often with a seventh or ninth added, or one of the other supertonic chords.

The chord is theoretically possible in sixteenth-century 'harmony' (so far as that term can be used in this connexion). Though, so far as the present writer can ascertain, there is no hint of it in the work of Palestrina or his school, the following passage from Byrd, quoted by Dr. Fellowes, seems to foreshadow it, especially when the rate of harmonic change is taken into account. It must, however, be realized, that such harmonic effects in this period were contrapuntal in origin.

A beautiful early example from Carissimi's *Jephtha* shows the chord used with complete assurance and moving effect on the word 'ululate'. The resolution is on the subdominant (first inversion).

In the work of Alessandro Scarlatti the full harmonic implications of the chord are realized. It is frequently found in the minor key, without any suggestion of modulation. Three examples quoted below give some idea of its effectiveness. In the first two the resolution is on dominant harmony via some passing notes (somewhat irregular in the first case). The third example shows resolutions on tonic and subdominant chords.

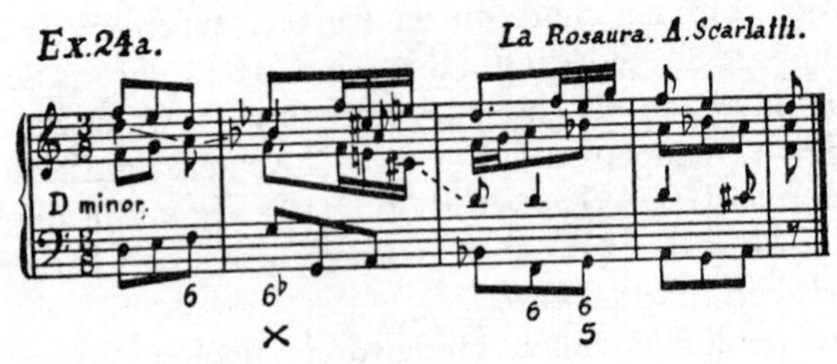

Bach made great use of the chord in its 'Neapolitan' form, generally in the minor key. Two memorable instances are quoted below, showing resolutions on dominant and supertonic chromatic harmony.

Ex. 25b. St Matthew Passion. No 33 Bach.

E minor.

An amazingly expressive example of the chord in a highly chromatic context in the major key (between a major triad on the flattened submediant and a diminished chord on the supertonic with a seventh added) shows Bach's great harmonic power. The chord is decorated with an accented passing note.

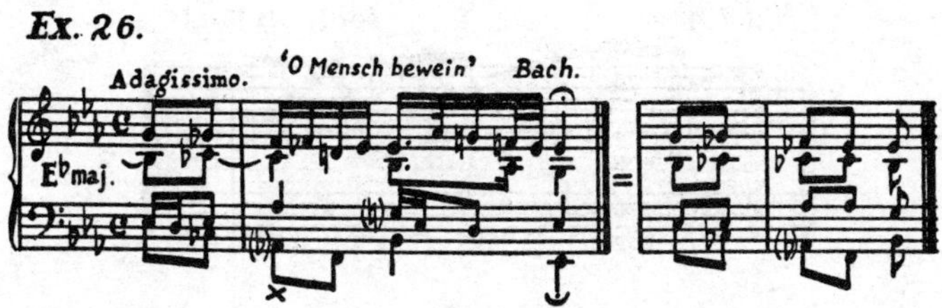

Bach produces some strange instances of the flat supertonic chord with a major seventh added. The effect is very harsh. The first example from the French suite in C minor is a sort of Neapolitan six-five resolving on the dominant. The second from the *C minor Partita* shows a second inversion.[1]

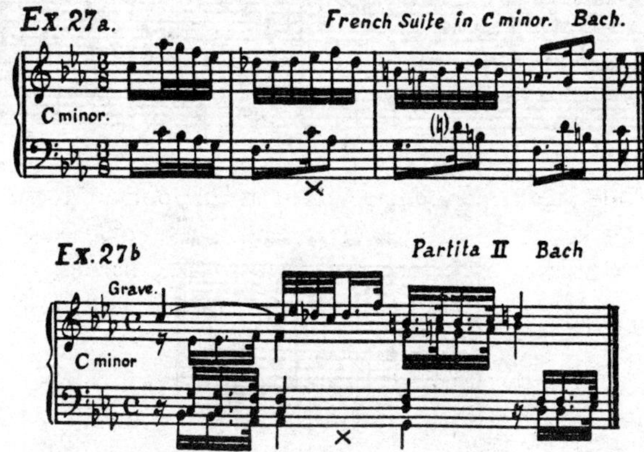

[1] A very striking example of the 'Neopolitan $^6_5$' is to be found in Beethoven: Symphony No. 3, 1st movement, eight bars before the first statement of the new 'theme' in E minor in the development section.

The Neapolitan sixth is sporadic in its appearances in Handel's work. When the chord is found it generally resolves on dominant harmony, and is usually in its normal form (first inversion) and in the minor key. The second example below seems to be a second inversion; in fact a Neapolitan $^6_4$. It is interesting, if not completely satisfying to some tastes.

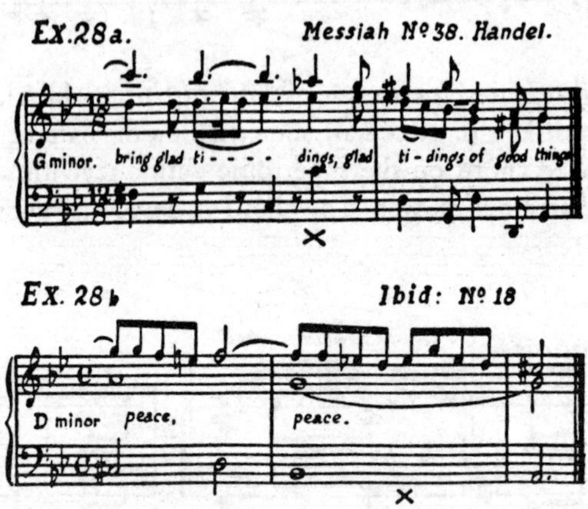

Handel's English contemporary, Greene, used the chord with a surer touch. Two very expressive examples, both resolving on tonic harmony, show this well.

Haydn employed the chord fairly frequently in modulation, but less often in the strictly chromatic way. Mozart on the other hand seems to have had a special liking for it.

Ex. 30 a
Piano Sonata in A minor. Mozart.
Allegro maestoso
A minor.

Ex. 30 b.
String Quartet : D minor. Mozart.
Allegro.
D minor.

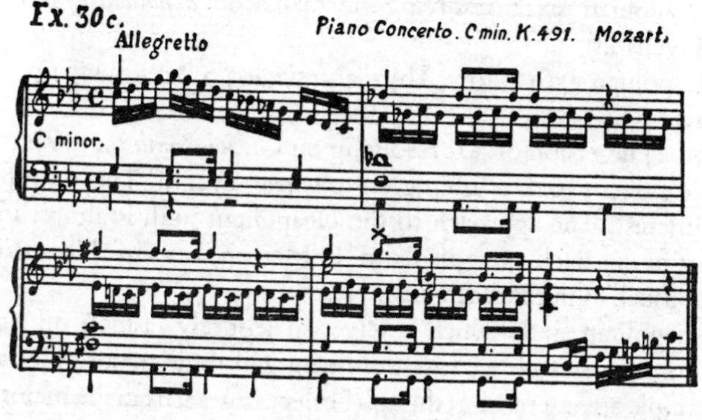
Ex. 30 c.
Allegretto
Piano Concerto. C min. K.491. Mozart.
C minor.

Ex. 30 d.
Allegro.
Clarinet Quintet. Mozart.
A major.

Ex. 30 e.
Piano Sonata XI. Haydn.
Allegro.
A (major.)

Notes on above examples

(a) Neapolitan sixth resolving normally on *dominant* minor ninth. (Third inversion)

(b) Neapolitan sixth followed by *root position of* ♭ II resolving on *dominant* harmony.

(c) *Second* inversion of ♭ II resolving on *German sixth* on ♭ VI.

(d) Neapolitan sixth resolving on *dominant* seventh. This example is of special interest. The approach to the Neapolitan sixth is almost identical with that in the Bach example from 'O Mensch, bewein'. The major key is also unusual, as in the Bach example.

(e) Neapolitan sixth which resolves in leisurely fashion on *supertonic chromatic* harmony followed by dominant and tonic major. This and the next example are interesting; though both passages start in the major mode, the minor mode appears before the Neapolitan sixth is used.

(f) Neapolitan sixth resolving on a *tonic minor* second inversion.

(g) Neapolitan sixth resolving on *supertonic* chromatic harmony.

Beethoven made impressive use of the chord, though its appearances in his work as a real chromatic chord are by no means common. Sometimes it is only hinted at, as in the first example cited below. The next two examples show the chord used above a pedal point, one in the major key. The fourth example shows the root position of ♭ II resolving directly upon a dominant seventh.

Schubert's frequent use of the chord is always very expressive. Three examples will be enough to show his characteristic procedure.

(a) A perfectly normal example of the Neapolitan sixth resolving on dominant harmony. It is worth noting that it forms an essential part of the melody.

(b) A root position of ♭ II resolving on a first inversion of VI. Also a normal Neapolitan sixth resolving on a tonic second inversion.

(c) A striking example of the Neapolitan sixth in the major key. The resolution is the normal one upon a tonic second inversion going to the dominant.

Brahms's work shows some interesting cases of ♭ II. The first example from the *Haydn Variations* contains the chord in root position followed by an Italian sixth on the same bass, resolving directly upon tonic harmony. The second a Neapolitan sixth in the major key resolving on the tonic chord.

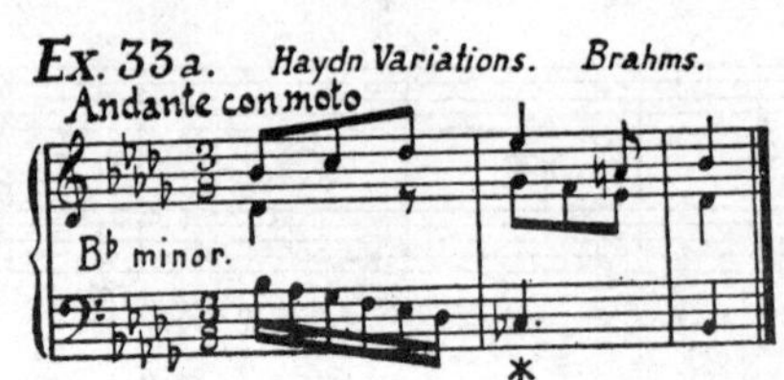

The examples which have been given should be enough to show the gradual development of the use of the major chord on ♭II from its beginning as little more than a mere passing note to its full importance as an integral part of melody and harmonic texture. The chord appears almost exclusively in the minor mode and generally in its first inversion in the seventeenth and eighteenth centuries. From the time of Beethoven onwards its use in the major mode and root position becomes much commoner. If the student has examined the passages quoted really carefully he should have little difficulty in using the chord in an appropriate way. It must be remembered that the chord has a strong character of its own, and it must be treated with caution and reserve, and kept for moments when its full effect is really appropriate.

Chapter Three

THE SUPERTONIC DIMINISHED TRIAD IN MAJOR KEYS

A DIMINISHED triad on the (diatonic) second degree of the (major) scale may be borrowed from the minor mode as a chromatic chord without modulation. A minor seventh can be added with good effect. The chord is generally found in its first inversion, and normally resolves on dominant or tonic harmony. This variant of supertonic harmony combines well with the other supertonic chords, and a resolution on the supertonic chromatic chord is quite common.

The following examples show the normal uses reduced to bare essentials.

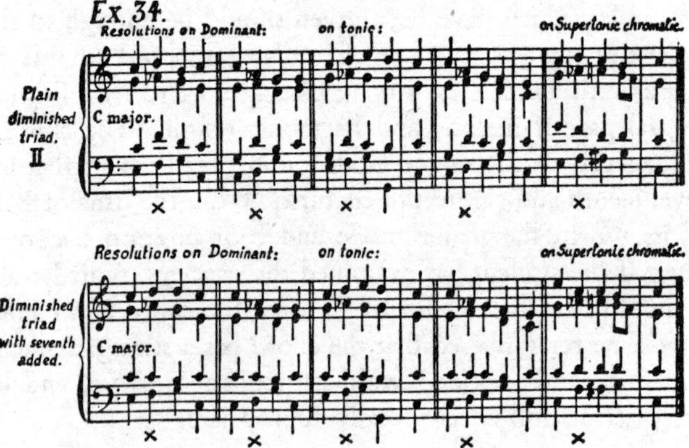

It is, of course, possible to regard the chord as part of a dominant discord; the dominant minor ninth (or eleventh) with the root and third omitted. In practice the effect of the chord is generally strongly supertonic, especially when the seventh is added. The first inversion with the seventh is equivalent to minor subdominant added sixth.

Turning to examples from actual music, it is evident that before the nineteenth century composers found little use for the chord in the strictly chromatic usage. The majority of Bach examples are very indefinite and have a strongly dominant flavour (diminished seventh on the leading note).

In Handel even such indefinite examples are rare. A Bach example already quoted comes reasonably near the mark if the harmonic analysis given beside it is accepted. (Example 35).

In the Mozart–Haydn period the appearances of the chord are little if any more convincing. It appears from time to time as a passing discord usually with a seventh added. Two examples will suffice to show this rather indefinite use. The Haydn example shows a second inversion (with the seventh) resolving on dominant harmony; the Mozart example, a third inversion again with the seventh, also resolving on the dominant; it is little more than a chromatic passing note added to a plain supertonic seventh.

Beethoven examples are very similar to those from Haydn and Mozart quoted above. The first example shows a close connexion with the supertonic chromatic chord, which here precedes a second inversion of the diminished chord with the seventh. The second example shows a passing use of the chord over a tonic pedal.

Two Schubert examples demonstrate a very much more definite treatment of the chord; Example 38a, the plain diminished triad in its first inversion resolving normally on the dominant; Example 38b, the diminished chord with a seventh in its first inversion resolving upon supertonic chromatic harmony.

The Romantic composers of the nineteenth century made much use of the chord. Four examples quoted below show the kind of thing that can be found in their work.

The Berlioz example shows the 'added sixth' form of the chord over a tonic pedal resolving on tonic harmony with a naïve but undoubtedly attractive result.

In the Schumann fragment a root position of the chord, plus the seventh, resolves normally on a dominant minor ninth. The contrast of these two chords is fairly convincing evidence against the theory that supertonic diminished chords are really dominant discords.

The example from a Mendelssohn organ sonata shows the root position of the chord, plus the seventh, resolving on supertonic chromatic harmony.

A first inversion of the plain diminished triad dressed in highly pianistic garb from a Chopin prelude resolves on a first inversion of the mediant chord. (Some people might like to think of it as a dominant thirteenth with nearly all the notes of that formidable chord omitted.)

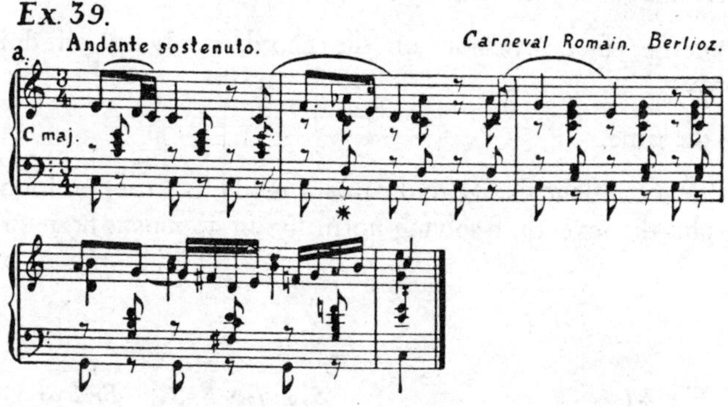

Brahms made frequent use of these chords. An example from the *Requiem* shows the diminished chord, plus the seventh, preceded by a tonic chromatic seventh resolving on tonic harmony over a tonic pedal.

An interesting piece of chromatic harmony in which the chord appears four times in eight bars is to be found in the third symphony. It is a good example of the extraordinary remoteness, and extension of the bounds of tonality which can be achieved by this means.

(a) is the first inversion of the diminished triad plus the seventh resolving on supertonic chromatic harmony.

(b) another first inversion of the chord, resolving on dominant harmony.

(c) is the same.

(d) after a transient change to the minor mode, is a root position of the chord, plus the seventh, resolving normally on dominant harmony.

Two more short examples which somehow remain in the memory, the one because it comes at the end of a great work, the other for its peculiar exotic flavour, are worth quoting. One is the added sixth type resolving on the tonic, the other a second inversion over a pedal.

From the examples given it may be seen that the supertonic diminished chords have in themselves not nearly so strong an individuality as the other chromatic variants already discussed. The plain diminished triad, as has been pointed out, has certain affinities with dominant discords, and the most usual position of the chord with the seventh added, the first inversion, has a strong minor subdominant (added sixth) character. The possibilities of the chord in root position should be carefully considered, for there it is most definite and probably most effective. The comparative rarity of its use except in the Romantic school suggests that composers have found it an unsatisfactory vehicle for expressing their thoughts except on rare occasions. It should be treated with the same reserve by the student.

Chapter Four

THE MINOR TRIAD ON THE SUBDOMINANT IN THE MAJOR KEYS

This variant of the subdominant chord borrowed from the minor key, can be used as a chromatic chord in the strict sense. Though it has acquired a bad reputation on account of its supposed attraction for the village organist, it can be quite strong and fine in its proper place.

If approached directly from the tonic it constitutes technically a temporary transition to the subdominant minor, though in many cases this is merely a theoretical change of key.

In other respects the chord may be treated simply as a variant of the diatonic subdominant triad. A minor seventh can be added to it with good effect.

Bach made use of the chord with his usual harmonic insight, though its appearances are rare. The first example shows a first inversion approached from submediant (A minor) harmony, resolving on a $^{6\,5}_{4\,3}$ on the dominant. The second example is a root position approached from the tonic and decorated with accented passing notes, resolving on the third inversion of a dominant seventh (which resolves rather strangely but effectively on supertonic chromatic harmony, the seventh in the bass rising).

An example from Handel shows one of the commonest uses of the chord. It may, of course, be regarded as implying some degree of modulation, but it has become so idiomatic that the feeling of modulation has almost entirely disappeared. It is merely the subdominant minor chord approached from the tonic over a tonic pedal.

In the Mozart–Haydn period the chord is found occasionally, but is usually little more than a passing chromaticism. The Mozart example below shows the first inversion approached from a tonic $^6_4$ resolving on supertonic chromatic harmony; it simply amounts to a chromatic passing note. In the Haydn example the chord is approached from the diatonic major form, and resolves on a dominant discord.

A fine example from Beethoven's *Hammerklavier* sonata shows the chord in its first inversion, decorated by a retardation, between two positions of tonic harmony. The Schubert quotation is harmonically similar with the subdominant minor chord in root position. Even though in this case it is dwelt upon there is no feeling of modulation. The effect is not the least moving part of one of the most moving passages in all chamber music.

Like the supertonic diminished chords, the Romantic composers seem to have found this minor version of the subdominant in the major keys attractive. Mendelssohn did not hesitate to use something very like the despised village organist formula in his Violin Concerto. The other examples are quite normal and clear. Chopin adds what is practically a major seventh (albeit a suspension) to the chord with good effect.

There is an interesting piece of chromatic harmony in Brahms's first symphony (slow movement): (1) is a tonic chromatic seventh resolving on (2) supertonic chromatic seventh (minus root) 3rd and 2nd inversions followed by (3) subdominant minor chord in first inversion resolving on (4) first inversion of the diminished chord on the supertonic. It is really one of those drifts of chromatic harmony of most effectively vague tonality, which will be considered later.

Brahms makes striking use of the hybrid tonality set up by the subdominant minor chord in the later *Variations on a theme by Handel*. The relevant passages are too long to quote, but the student is advised to look at the variation beginning as follows and the one which comes after it (variations 23 and 24).

Grieg's piano concerto slow movement provides a well-known example of the chord plus a minor seventh between two statements of the tonic chord. It may be noted that the presence of the seventh in the subdominant minor chord removes any possible feeling of modulation.

There is a fine example of the chord in *Nimrod* (Elgar: *Enigma Variations*). It appears in its second inversion as a passing $\frac{6}{4}$ between two statements of dominant harmony.

An example, from the end of the first movement of Sibelius's second symphony, of the chord resolving on dominant harmony over a tonic pedal may serve to show that it still has its uses.

From these examples it may be seen that the subdominant minor chord used as a chromatic harmony in the major mode, despite its inherent weakness, has its place in the harmonic vocabulary. The most interesting quality of the chord lies, perhaps, in its capacity for creating something like a new scale, as the Brahms examples suggest. More will be said on this point in a later chapter.

Chapter Five

THE TONIC CHROMATIC CHORD

It is hard to contemplate the tonic minor chord in the major key, or the tonic major chord in the minor key, as chromatic harmony without modulation or at least transitory change of mode. There are, however, certain uses which, though not chromatic in the strictest sense, are important.

The very common use of the tonic major triad as the final chord of a work or section in the minor key, the 'tierce de Picardie', has been common property from the Polyphonic period, when it was the rule, to the present day. It necessarily implies a change from the minor to the major key in modern tonality.

The alternation of the major and minor tonic chords can produce a remarkable atmosphere of restlessness or suspense. Two well-known examples will illustrate this. The process of course involves temporary change of mode.

Beethoven gets much nearer to a strictly chromatic use of tonic chromatic triads in the following passages. The first two from the *Mass in D* show the first inversion of a minor triad on the tonic resolving on dominant harmony. These are very definite examples with no suggestion of modulation, nor can they be entirely explained away as chromatic passing notes. The third passage, from the *Hammerklavier* sonata, shows a first inversion of the tonic minor chord in the major key resolving on the supertonic. In the last example the major chord on the tonic resolves on supertonic harmony, both chords being in their first inversions.

THE TONIC CHROMATIC SEVENTH

The tonic major chord with a *minor* seventh added may be used as a chromatic chord in the strict sense in both major and minor keys. If it is followed directly by subdominant harmony it suggests modulation since it is the dominant seventh of the subdominant key. It can, however, be resolved upon dominant or some form of supertonic harmony without implied modulation.

Reduced to the simplest terms, the following examples show the normal resolutions.

Ex. 56.

Resolutions: on Dominant. on Supertonic. on Supertonic chromatic. on Neapolitan sixth.

Resolutions: on Dominant on Supertonic. on Supertonic chromatic. on Neapolitan sixth.

In this rudimentary form it might seem that the chord has small musical possibilities. The resolutions on a dominant discord or supertonic chromatic chord are unduly crude. Those on the plain supertonic or supertonic seventh are more promising, and the Neapolitan sixth resolution seems to hold the most musical answer to the problem.

A fairly extensive examination of examples from actual music will show what composers could do with the chord.

In Purcell's work there are many cases which seem to point to a possible origin of the chord. The following passages are obviously strongly influenced by the Mixo-lydian mode. In both cases the tonic seventh resolves on a chord on the flat seventh of the scale. The effect is most beautiful.

A splendid example of the last inversion of the chord resolving on a second inversion of a supertonic seventh comes from Purcell's magnificent eight-part setting of the first verse of Psalm 102. It might be argued that the B♭ in the bass is merely a passing note, but at the very least the passage shows the origin of one of the standard uses of the chord.

Bach used the chord very freely, generally bringing about a transient modulation to the subdominant. The passage quoted below is typical of one of his most common harmonic devices.

Prout quotes four examples of strict chromatic usage from Bach. Of these two seem completely convincing; the first quoted below is a second inversion of the tonic seventh resolving on a third inversion of a dominant minor ninth; the second is the same position of the tonic seventh resolving in the same way, over a dominant pedal.

The next three Bach examples show resolutions on supertonic harmony. The third, from one of the most moving choral preludes he ever wrote, seems particularly satisfying.

A resolution on a second inversion of a supertonic chromatic ninth occurs in the great organ fugue in C major.

An unusual resolution of the chord on a submediant seventh is both interesting and effective.

Examples of the chord in Handel's work are rare. Prout quotes a good instance of the third inversion in the minor key resolving on supertonic chromatic harmony.

After the Bach–Handel period the chord as a purely chromatic chord becomes rarer in its appearance. It remains, however, one of the most frequently used methods of modulation to the subdominant.

Of the real chromatic examples, one from Haydn, resolving on a Neapolitan sixth is worth noticing for its beauty.

The Mozart example below is a perfectly normal resolution on the supertonic.

Prout's Beethoven quotation of a root position of the tonic chromatic seventh resolving on a dominant seventh also in root position, is interesting, though it cannot claim to be an example without suggested modulation. The whole passage shows a modulation from D minor to C major. although the part quoted by Prout (shown in square brackets) might well be in C major throughout. It is an interesting if rather difficult use of the chord, not wholly satisfying to some minds.

Another Beethoven example will show a more normal use of the chord resolving on an inversion of dominant harmony.

A fine Schubert example comes from the beginning of the *Death and the Maiden* quartet. The tonic chromatic seventh here resolves on a Neapolitan sixth. The whole passage is an interesting prolonged stretch of chromatic harmony.

Brahms makes some use of the chord in the strictly chromatic sense. The first quotation below shows a resolution on supertonic chromatic harmony. The end of the passage has already been cited in an earlier chapter and the harmony analysed there (p. 33). The second example takes us back to the Bach formula shown in Example 59. Brahms like Bach was very fond of this harmonic idiom. In this case there is really no feeling of modulation to the subdominant after the first statement of the chord, and the resolution on a dominant discord is in keeping with a strict chromatic usage.

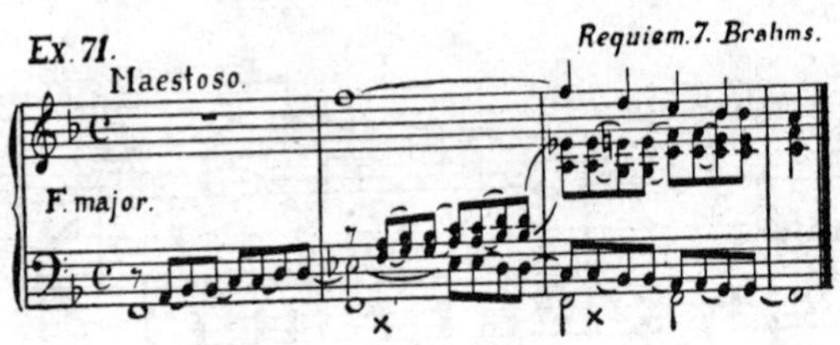

A final example from Wagner shows the chord over a tonic pedal resolving first on a decorated supertonic triad and later on a dominant minor ninth.

TONIC CHROMATIC NINTHS

A major or minor ninth can be added to the tonic chromatic seventh, and used either as an essential note or accented passing note (or appoggiatura). The commonest form is the minor ninth with the root omitted in an inversion; in other words the diminished seventh derived from the tonic chromatic harmony.

For purposes of modulation these ninths are frequently found, especially the diminished seventh form. As strictly chromatic chords they are rare and rather obscure. The normal treatment of the ninth will be the same as in the case of dominant or supertonic chromatic ninths.

It is scarcely necessary to add a long string of examples of what is after all little more than a decoration of the tonic chromatic seventh already cited. Clear cases of the ninth used in the strictly chromatic way are few, and this would make anything like historical treatment well-nigh impossible. One memorable passage from Beethoven's *Diabelli Variations* may be quoted. There is no real feeling of key change throughout the passage.

Chapter Six

CHORDS OF THE AUGMENTED SIXTH

CHORDS of the augmented sixth differ from the chromatic chords discussed so far in that they are not diatonic in any key. They are of great value in modulation, and are in themselves chords of strong individuality. Much use has been made of them as purely chromatic chords without modulation, although the inherent quality of two basic harmonies superimposed creates some problems of ambiguity of key when the chords are used thus.

AUGMENTED SIXTHS ON THE FLATTENED SUBMEDIANT

Augmented sixths are most commonly met with on the flattened submediant of the scale. Three forms, called for no very clear reason, 'Italian', 'German', and 'French', are the most usual.

The text-book definition of these chords as 'chords with two roots,' however unsatisfactory from an acoustical point of view, has this to be said for it, that it does explain to some extent the dual personality of the harmony. They are, theoretically, 'supertonic chromatic plus dominant' discords. The following diagram may explain their family tree.

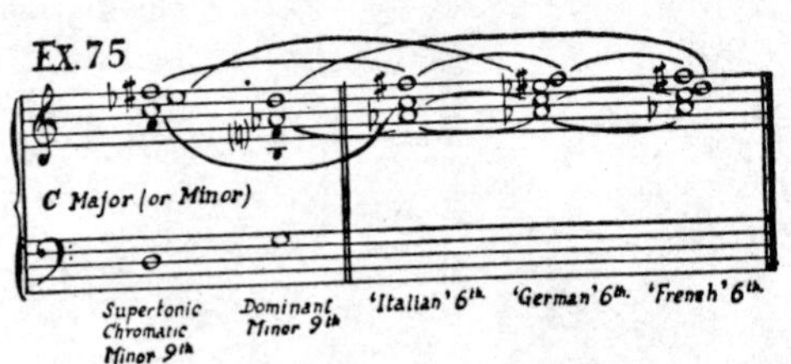

The supertonic chromatic element is the strongest factor in the Italian and German forms. Dominant and supertonic chromatic come nearer to sharing the honours in the French, although the supertonic still wins. These origins point to the normal resolutions of the chords, the most usual, as with the supertonic chromatic chords, being on a dominant discord or some position of the tonic harmony.

Before considering the possibilities of these chords without modulation, it is necessary to find out how far such progressions as the following imply inherent change of key.

As in the case of supertonic chromatic harmony resolving on the plain dominant chord it may be held that a temporary transition to the dominant has been made in both these cases and that in order to avoid all suggestion of modulation this resolution must be on a dominant *discord*. As was pointed out in dealing with the supertonic chromatic chord, the modulation is usually merely theoretical, and in point of fact it is by no means easy to establish the dominant key in this way. This will become even more evident when the augmented sixths on the flat supertonic are investigated. The only real test of whether modulation has taken place or not is the impression made by the passage as a whole in performance. In the Beethoven example it would be absurd to say that a shift of key centre to B♭ has taken place. Almost equally absurd would be the suggestion of a modulation to G major in the Mozart example.

The origin of these chords may be traced back to Byrd's 'extreme sharp sixth'. It must be remembered that such harmonic effects as these are in origin nothing more than the incidental contingency of the behaviour of melodic lines at a given point. It is clear that, as Dr. Fellowes so well points out, Byrd was attracted by the result of this particular combination for a time. Four examples appear in the two books of *Cantiones Sacrae*. (See also Example 115.)

Dr. Fellowes quotes another excellent example from Wilbye's *My throat is sore* (No. 27, Set I).

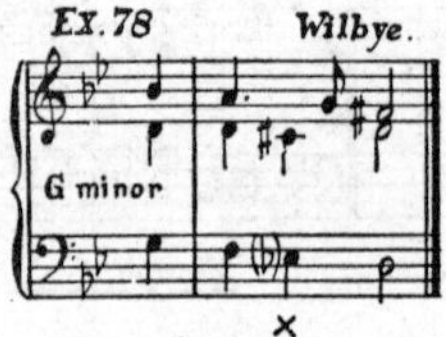

More unexpected is the appearance of the chord in the Italian school of the sixteenth century. Morris quotes a very remarkable passage from Lassus in which the augmented sixth is vouched for by Sandberger (editor-in-chief of the Breitkopf edition of Lassus). Lassus, like the English composers of the period, was fond of using chromaticisms for the purpose of realistic illustration, and it is this tendency coupled in some cases with an obvious seeking after greater means of emotional expression which probably accounts for most of the chromatic experiment of the time.

This Lassus example is much less definite in its key implications than those of the English school already quoted. It is nevertheless extremely interesting.

An interesting early example[1] in a more definitely harmonic texture is to be found in Monteverdi's *Orfeo*. Here again the object seems to be the expression of intense emotion.

[1] It must be stated here that although Malipiero accepts the G♯ over the B♭ bass, this interpretation is open to some doubt. The Sandberger Facsimile shows the ♯ sign written before each of the first two 'G's but not before the third. On the other hand a change from a sharp to a natural in such passages is usually corrected by a cancelling sign.

Not much progress was made in the use of the augmented sixths during the seventeenth century. Appearances are rare and rather vague. A fairly clear Purcell example shows one of the normal uses of later times more than hinted at. A Blow example on the flat supertonic will be given later. A surprising example from a Kuhnau clavier suite, in which, if the text is correct, the augmented and major sixths appear simultaneously, is worth quoting. These examples are included simply on account of their interest in the development of the use of the chord.

Handel used the chords very sparingly even in modulation. There seems to be only one definite augmented sixth in the *Messiah*, and four in *Israel in Egypt*. Two examples given below, both in the minor key, appear

to show uncertainty in handling the chords. The first is an Italian sixth approached from the submediant chord resolving on the dominant; the second a German sixth approached from the chord on the (melodic) minor seventh degree of the scale resolving on the dominant. In both cases the augmented sixth is doubled!

Many striking examples of the chords are to be found in Bach, all the more telling on account of the comparative rarity of their employment, at any rate as strictly chromatic harmonies. He seems to have realized their strong individuality and to have kept them for special moments. Three examples quoted below show (a) the Italian form approached from a supertonic seventh, and resolving on dominant harmony; (b) the German form (much the most common in Bach) approached from a seventh on the submediant, and resolving on supertonic chromatic harmony; (c) the French form, resolved normally as (a). It may be observed that most of the examples found in Bach, at least in the strictly chromatic use, seem to be in the minor keys.

The normal tendency of the parts responsible for the augmented interval to move outwards by step is well seen in (a). (b) shows an equally satisfactory behaviour of the discordant elements, one rising a semitone (the root), the other remaining stationary (the augmented sixth). At (c) the root falls a semitone, and the sixth is left to look after itself (quite a normal proceeding in instrumental music).

In the Haydn–Mozart period the use of the chords without modulation becomes so common as to be almost a mannerism. In Haydn the Italian form is the most usual, sometimes with decoration of the third giving a slight French sixth flavour. The German form is much less common, and the real French form rare, the example quoted being typical of its transient appearances.

It is of interest to notice that, like the Neapolitan sixth, the chords begin to appear in the major keys at this period.

The first Haydn example is of an Italian sixth approached from and resolving on dominant harmony; the second is the German form approached from a supertonic chromatic ninth and resolving on a tonic $^6_4$; the third a near approach to the French form following a first inversion of a minor subdominant seventh resolving on a dominant seventh.

Three very clear-cut Mozart examples are given below. The first an Italian sixth approached direct from the tonic, resolving on a plain dominant chord. The second a German sixth approached in the same way, resolving on a tonic $^6_4$. The third a French sixth turning into a submediant seventh resolving on a tonic $^6_4$.

A very remarkable passage from the well-known Mozart C major Quartet is worth careful study. Whatever it may look like on paper, the sound of the whole passage is definitely F major. It is a fine example of extending the bounds of tonality within the key, by means of unessential chromatic notes as well as chromatic chords. It also illustrates the dual personality of the augmented sixths, in the key uncertainty of bars 4 and 5 (F major, C major?), which eventually settles itself quite definitely in bar 6 in F major. The inverted pedal F in the first four bars is worth noting; it binds the passage together most effectively.

Beethoven used augmented sixths freely, often with great emotional effect. The following examples show the three forms, and need no explanation, save to point out that the E♮ in the third quotation is equivalent to an F♭; it is merely what theorists call 'expedient false notation' and is commonly found as an alternative spelling of the German sixth.

Schubert used the chords in much the same way as Beethoven, usually at moments of emotional stress. The approach from the tonic and normal resolution is generally found. Three clear examples are given below.

During the nineteenth century the augmented sixths passed into the normal vocabulary of chromatic chords, though they were not so frequently employed by the Romantic composers as might be expected. In the case of the chords in root position without modulation little was added to the procedures already described. Brahms was very fond of the chords and they are a characteristic feature of his harmony. His treatment of them is usually quite normal, as the following examples will show.

INVERSIONS OF AUGMENTED SIXTHS ON THE FLAT SUBMEDIANT

All inversions of all three forms of the chord are theoretically possible.

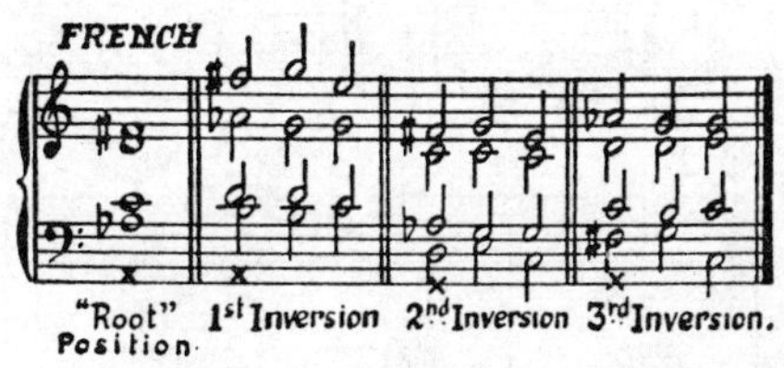

The inversions of the Italian form are very rare and not particularly satisfactory. The two discordant elements are emphasized in inversion, and the result is inclined to sound thin and crude.

It should be realized that augmented sixth chords are considerably altered in effect by inversion. The augmented sixth from the bass, which gives the essential character to the chord in root position, is lost in the process.

The German sixth is much more useful in its inversions. The third inversion has a long and noble history, and the first inversion is very effective. The second inversion is less satisfactory.

The French form inverts well in all positions. It contains more discordant elements than the other sixths, and sounds almost like a completely different chord in some inversions.

The examples given below may perhaps suffice to show most of the accepted uses of inversions of augmented sixths on the flat submediant. Their use in classical times is rare. Bach with his tremendous harmonic powers could handle them in masterly fashion. Beethoven and Schubert found in them a powerful means of expression. The later nineteenth-century composers used them with varying degrees of success, and sometimes, it must be said, with unpleasantly cloying results. (César Franck and Wolf are by no means blameless in this respect.)

CHORDS OF THE AUGMENTED SIXTH

INVERSIONS OF AUGMENTED SIXTHS ON THE FLAT SUBMEDIANT.

SECOND INVERSIONS.

Prout points out that though the Italian, German and French forms of the augmented sixth are by far the most common, they are 'by no means the only ones to be found'. He quotes the famous Tristan example and regards the G♯ as an essential note. This is quite a possible explanation, though in view of the prevalence of chromatic appoggiaturas in the style, and the sound of the passage taken as a whole, one may doubt the correctness of this view, and simply regard the G♯ as a long appoggiatura of the A.

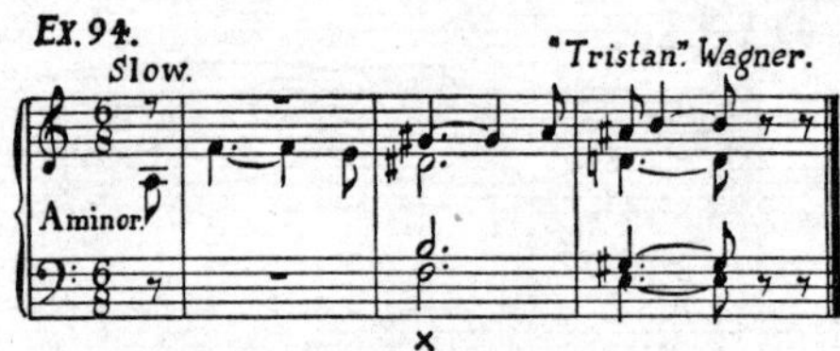

His example of the same form of the chord from the opening of Haydn's *Creation* is much more convincing. It is an augmented sixth on the flat

submediant with an augmented fourth and augmented second (or minor third by altered spelling) in its first inversion. In fact it is the Tristan chord without any doubt about the augmented second's legitimacy. It should be studied carefully, as a very interesting and, at the time, daring piece of chromatic harmony.

Prout also gives a fine variant from the Verdi *Requiem*. This time the augmented sixth on the flat submediant in root position is accompanied by a major third and augmented fifth.

It is, of course, possible to explain the C♮ in the bass as a chromatic passing note.

AUGMENTED SIXTHS ON THE FLATTENED SUPERTONIC

All three usual forms of the augmented sixth are found on the minor second of the scale. The theoretician's explanation of the chords requires simultaneous dominant and tonic roots. The genealogical table is quite clear.

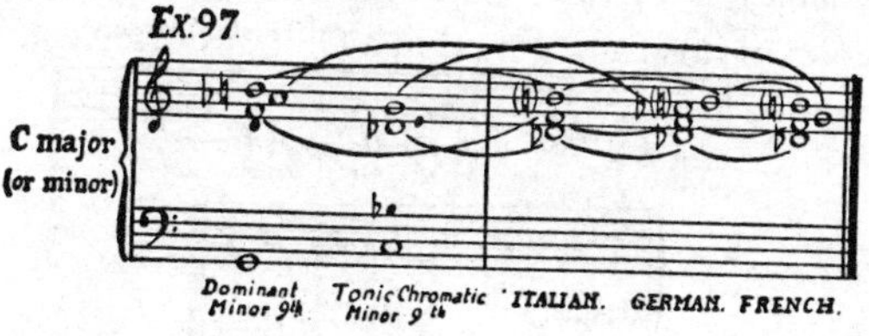

The dominant origin is obviously the stronger element in the chords. Yet a straightforward resolution on tonic harmony is by no means a definite cadence in the tonic key. The tonic chromatic element in the chords is strong enough to suggest the subdominant key, and it is not easy to make the tonic chord in this resolution sound convincing as a tonic chord. The progression sounds more like a half close in the subdominant.

Other resolutions are on a dominant discord, or possibly some form of supertonic or chromatic supertonic harmony.

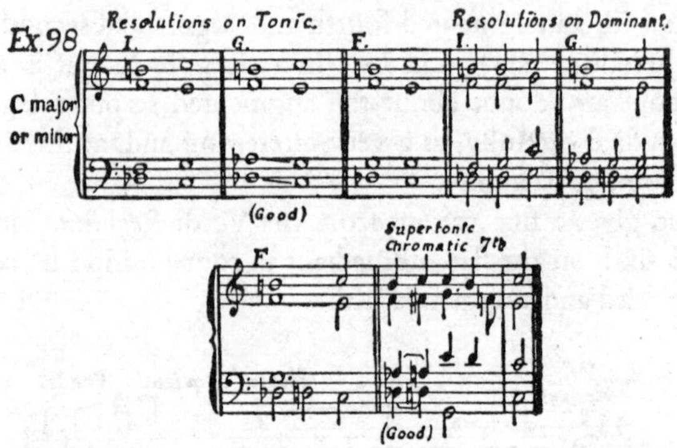

Turning to examples from real music, the use of augmented sixths on the flat supertonic as chromatic chords without modulation is rare. The tendency for modulation to the subdominant key is always present to some extent, and really definite examples are hard to find. As in the case of the chords on the flat submediant, the context and musical effect of the whole passage have to be taken into account, and individual judgment must play some part in determining the authenticity of each example.

The comparative rarity of the chords on this degree of the scale makes historical treatment such as has been attempted in previous chapters difficult and unprofitable. The examples which follow are, it is hoped, for the most part fairly straightforward. Though far from complete as a set of illustrations, they may serve to show some of the possibilities of the three forms of the augmented sixth on the flat supertonic.

The Italian form is very rare. Curiously enough one of the most satisfactory examples of it is to be found in a Gibbons madrigal.

A much less definite case is seen in Blow's magnificent motet, *Salvator Mundi*. It illustrates the purely contrapuntal origin of most harmony of this kind. (Example 100).

An interesting pair of examples from Bach and Handel, almost a complete parallel usage, again shows the passing note origin of these chords.

One further example of the Italian form must suffice. Beethoven uses the chord preceded by the tonic, resolving on a dominant discord.

The German form on the flat supertonic is less rare. A fine Bach example, resolving on a tonic chord decorated with a $\frac{6}{4}$ suspension, shows a definite and regular use.

A much more tentative Haydn specimen, illustrating very clearly the passing note origin of the chord, is worth quoting as an interesting piece of chromatic harmony. (A) Tonic first inversion; (B) supertonic chromatic seventh; (C) dominant minor ninth second inversion turning into (D) German sixth on flat supertonic; (E) subdominant minor triad, second inversion; (F) dominant seventh first inversion.

A Mozart example shows the chord resolving on the tonic after the upper three notes have been suspended over a tonic bass. It might be argued that the passage is really in D minor, but on the whole it seems best to regard the F natural as a chromatic note, at (A) suggesting the minor subdominant chord and at (B) the chord on the flat supertonic, thinking of the whole as in A major. This example is included partly because it shows the blending of two tonalities to which chromatic harmony gives rise, and the difficulty of deciding upon the real key of such passages.

Two examples, the first from Beethoven's Quartet Op. 18, No. 1, the second from Schubert's great C major symphony, show the chord resolving directly on the tonic.

Lastly, a splendid use from Sibelius in conjunction with a 'pedal' E♭ on the horns. The chord here is preceded by a minor chord on the sub-dominant plus a minor seventh.

The French form of the chord on the flat supertonic is rare in classical harmony, but its appearances are usually very impressive. The following passage from Beethoven shows the chord resolving on a dominant discord.

The wonderful ending of Schubert's string *Quintet* provides an instance of a resolution directly on to the tonic.

Equally memorable is Brahms's use of the chord in the opening statement of the *Passacaglia* in the fourth symphony. The sombre colouring of the passage with the heavy brass chords reaches its emotional climax on this French sixth resolved upon a tonic chord with 'tierce de Picardie'.

Finally a very impressive moment from the closing scene of *Götterdämmerung*. The resolution again employs the 'tierce de Picardie'.

INVERSIONS OF AUGMENTED SIXTHS ON THE FLAT SUPERTONIC

All the inversions of the augmented sixths on the flat supertonic are theoretically possible, but except with modulation they are very rarely found. A few examples of the German form which are reasonably convincing are given below.

SECOND INVERSION.

THIRD INVERSION.

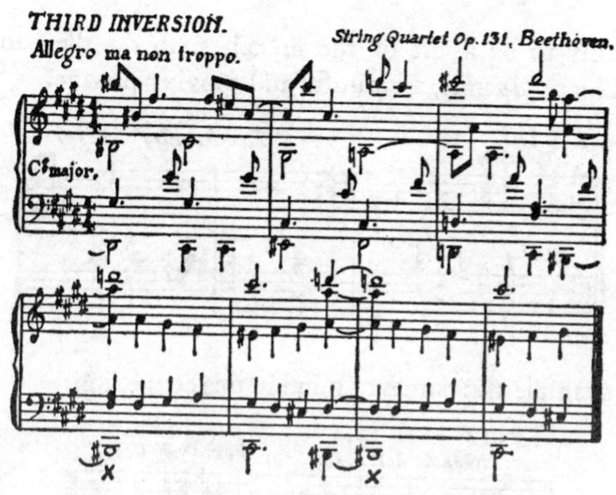

AUGMENTED SIXTHS ON OTHER DEGREES OF THE SCALE

The possibility of augmented sixths on the subdominant of the scale without modulation must not be overlooked. To describe the chord in C major as a selection of notes from dominant harmony with the fifth sharpened is grotesque.

Ex. 113.

An example from Brahms's string *Quintet in G* gives food for thought. (German form)

Curiously enough, Byrd brought about much the same effect, though admittedly by contrapuntal means. (Italian form)

What seems to be a use of the French sixth on the subdominant appears in Elgar's *Apostles*, a beautiful and moving passage.

A Grieg example also comes to mind in this connexion.

The French form of the augmented sixth can undergo a very subtle enharmonic change in its second inversion and reappear as a new and normal French sixth on a bass note an augmented fourth higher.

The chords produced by this method, French sixths on the supertonic and dominant degrees of the scale, are of course valueless as chromatic harmonies in music constructed on the diatonic scale system, being in fact mere misspellings. Their possibilities in the whole tone system are obvious. In the diatonic system they seem to have considerable potential usefulness in enharmonic modulation, though from an acoustical point of view the complications would probably be enormous.

Although this part of the book is concerned with the use of chromatic chords without modulation, it may not be out of place to quote one example of this very involved process here. The notation has been simplified and the enharmonic change shown. The chord marked × from the F minor angle is a French sixth on the submediant (D♭), first heard in its last (third) inversion and then in its second inversion. From the F♯ minor angle it is a French sixth on the flat supertonic (G♮) in its first inversion and root position. Despite the complication of the technical explanation the effect is perfectly clear and natural.

Chapter Seven

AUGMENTED FIFTHS (MAJOR KEYS)

DURING the Classical period, dominant harmony with the fifth sharpened came into considerable use. The text-book explanation of the chord is that it is a dominant minor thirteenth, changed enharmonically. Whatever may be its real harmonic origin, it is fairly clear that it grew out of the alteration of the fifth of the dominant chord by means of a chromatic passing note, which eventually became self-sufficient. The normal crude form of the chord and its resolution look most unpleasant in cold blood. (Some examples later will show what composers actually did with it.)

The augmented fifth has a strong tendency to rise a semitone; this should be indulged. It quarrels violently with the seventh if sounded below it.

The chromatic passing note origin is clearly seen in the following Mozart and Beethoven examples. In the first the dominant seventh in its first inversion is decorated with a chromatically sharpened fifth. In the second the plain chord is similarly treated. In the third a root position of the dominant seventh has the same decoration.

Two further Beethoven quotations show the chord standing much more in its own right. The first is a particularly clear example of this; in it Beethoven moves directly to a dominant seventh with the fifth sharpened. In the second the chord is approached from plain dominant harmony, but here it has the effect of almost a new chord.

Schubert made striking use of the augmented fifth. In *Die Krahe* from *Winterreise* its effect is unforgettable. A 'passing' example from the great C major Symphony is also worth notice.

Brahms also made good use of the chord, both in the direct way, as a quotation from the late string quintet illustrates, and in the passing note idiom.

Augmented fifths became a very important factor in Wagner's harmony. Two short passages from the *Siegfried Idyll* will illustrate (a) the normal use with the dominant chord over a tonic pedal, and (b) the principle of sharpening the fifth applied to another of the primary triads. (More will be said of this later.)

In Dvořák's work the augmented fifth dominant chord becomes almost a mannerism. A typical example is quoted below.

It is possible to treat other basic chords in this way. An augmented fifth can be substituted for the normal fifth in the tonic, subdominant and supertonic chromatic harmonies. The inversions of the resulting chords, treated enharmonically, give all the augmented fifths possible on the piano.

It will be seen that the chords marked * in Example 125 (b) may be regarded as enharmonically changed versions of the tonic chord with the fifth sharpened.

Any extensive use of the results of this harmonic procedure inevitably tends towards the adoption of the whole tone scale. This scale is outside the range of the present book, but it is necessary to mention it in this connexion.

The whole tone scale combines uneasily with diatonic tonality. Debussy found in it many possibilities for the expression of his musical ideas, and did succeed to some extent in reconciling it with traditional diatonic tonality. It is, however, generally admitted that the whole tone scale system is a by-way which leads away from the main path of musical development. It is furthermore a very restricted system; even more restricted than the modal system from the view point of tonality. It seems doubtful whether there is more to be said in it than has already been said by the French impressionists.

A restricted use of augmented fifth chords for purposes of modulation within the diatonic key system is perfectly valid. It is doubtful whether their use as strictly chromatic chords can be taken much further than has already been suggested in this chapter.

Chapter Eight

OTHER CHROMATIC CHORDS

During the last hundred years or so composers have turned their attention more and more to the possibilities of chromatic triads and sevenths on degrees of the scale other than those already discussed. These chromatic variants include some harmonic effects within the key of very great beauty and interest. A short survey of some of these chords may show the way to even wider harmonic resources.

CHROMATIC TRIADS AND SEVENTHS ON THE SUBMEDIANT

(1) *The Major Common Chord on the Flat Submediant in the Major Key*

This beautiful chord has a long and distinguished history. Bach's

splendid use of it as an approach to the Neapolitan sixth (already much quoted) has been followed by later composers. (Example 128).

Prout quotes an interesting example from Schubert showing the chord in root position and second inversion, in both cases resolving on tonic harmony.

Brahms was obviously fond of the chord and it appears very frequently in his works. The first two examples show it plus a passing note major seventh in root position and first inversion resolving on supertonic chromatic harmony. In the third the chord resolves on a diminished seventh of supertonic chromatic origin over a tonic pedal. The fourth example shows the chord in root position resolving first on the tonic and later on the subdominant minor triad.

In a very beautiful passage from Debussy's string quartet the chord is used over a tonic pedal between two statements of supertonic harmony.

A passage from Elgar illustrates the use of the chord over a dominant pedal, resolving on dominant harmony.

In the last movement of Sibelius's second symphony there is a fine example of the chord with the major seventh resolving on an augmented sixth.

(2) *The Minor Triad on the Flattened Submediant*

This is a much more recent development. It is a very striking chord indeed, and in the major key every note is chromatic. It must be reserved for very special moments. The normal resolution will be on tonic or dominant harmony.

(3) *The Major Common Chord on the (Major) Submediant*

A form of this chord with the minor seventh added in its first inversion, used without modulation, was idiomatic in the classical period. The resolution on the dominant was normally employed. The following examples will show the process. The passage from Beethoven Op 59, No. 3, contains the chord in root position as well as in the first inversion.

The use of the plain major triad seems to be a much later development.[1] It has a completely different flavour. Whereas the classical idiom is only successful in the major key, the plain chord can be used equally well in the minor key. A few examples will indicate the possibilities of what is

[1] A sixteenth-century origin may, however, be traced.

of necessity a highly colourful chromatic harmony and therefore one rarely used.

CHROMATIC CHORDS ON THE SEVENTH DEGREE OF THE SCALE

The possibilities of chromatic chords on the seventh degree are very considerable.

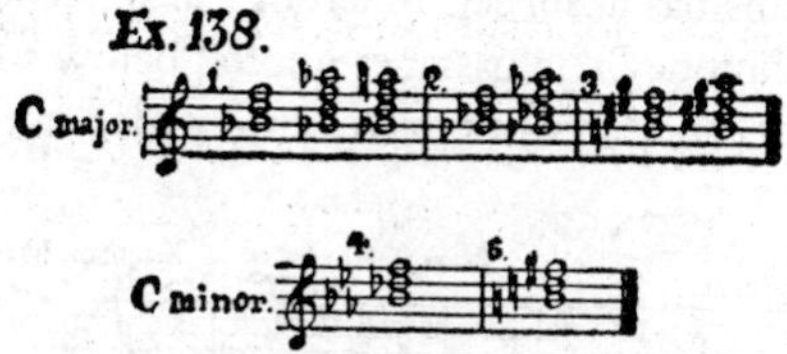

(1) *The Major Chord on the Flattened Seventh Degree*

This is definitely a chord of modal origin. It is a common and very beautiful part of sixteenth-century technique. The following illustrations will make its use perfectly clear.

The modal feeling of the chord is so strong that it can hardly be used as a chromatic harmony in modern tonality without conscious modal effect.

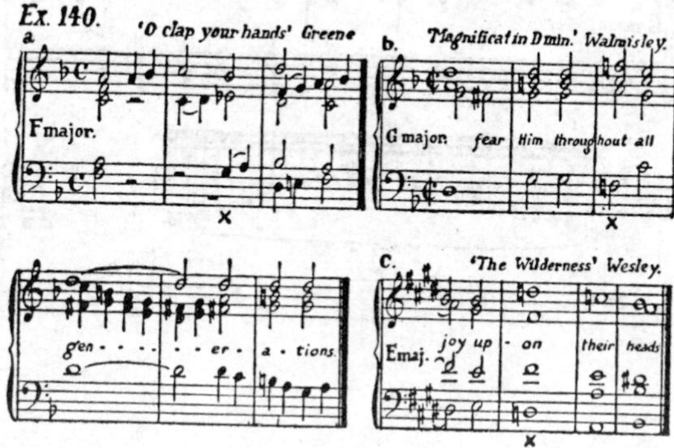

The modal feeling survived to some extent right through the tradition of English cathedral music. It is not surprising, therefore, to find this chord employed quite naturally with no feeling of anachronism in English church music of many periods. Three examples from eighteenth- and nineteen-century church composers will demonstrate this. (The last two, well-quoted by Kitson, are very typical, and exceedingly effective.) (Ex. 140).

Vaughan Williams has absorbed much of the sixteenth-century modal feeling into his technique. The passages quoted below show his use of the chord, with a major, and later minor, seventh added in the second case.

(2) *The Minor Triad (with a possible Seventh) on the Flattened Leading Note*

A good example can be found in Rimsky-Korsakov's *Scheherazade*. The chord with a minor seventh added appears between two statements of tonic harmony.

(3) *The Major Common Chord (with a possible Seventh) on the Leading Note*

This chord may be used in the strictly chromatic way resolving on the dominant or tonic.

(4) *The Minor Triad on the Flattened Seventh Degree of the Minor Scale*

This chord is difficult to use without a feeling of modulation. The opening of the Prelude to Debussy's *La Damoiselle Élue* shows the most natural and musical progression available.

(5) *The Minor Triad on the Leading Note (Sharpened Seventh) of the Minor Scale*

This remarkably effective chord seems to be very rarely used. An admirable example between two statements of a dominant seventh may be found in Dvořak's second symphony.

CHROMATIC CHORDS ON THE THIRD DEGREE OF THE SCALE

Two chromatic chords on the mediant must be considered.

(1) *The Major Common Chord (and Seventh) on the Mediant*

This chord has classical authority behind it. It plays a notable part in the fifth movement of Beethoven's C♯ minor quartet.

A Berlioz example has a suggestion of modulation to F♯ minor, but that key is never established, and at the pace the effect is that of a chromatic chord.

A very striking example comes from Verdi's *Requiem.* The chord is sandwiched between two tonic chords.

The quotation from the Brahms *Requiem* shows the chord between two statements of the dominant seventh.

From Fauré's *Requiem* comes an example of the chord with the minor seventh added, following the same harmonic scheme as that of Brahms.

(2) *The Major Common Chord on the Flattened Mediant*

This chord is, of course, diatonic in the minor keys. In the major keys it is highly chromatic. Four examples are given below. The first shows the chord in root position resolving on a major chord on the flat submediant with a major seventh added. The second quotation gives a wonderful sense of remoteness; the chord is in its first inversion. In the third, the chord resolves on a diatonic mediant triad. The example from Ravel's *Sonatina* shows the second inversion between two statements of tonic harmony.

CHROMATIC CHORDS ON THE FIFTH DEGREE OF THE SCALE

Three chromatic chords on the dominant make occasional appearances as real chromatic harmony.

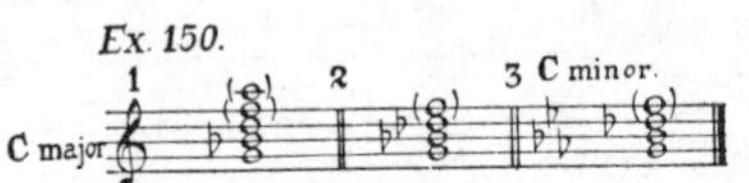

(1) *The Minor Triad (with the possible addition of a Seventh and Ninth) on the Dominant*

There is a good example with a seventh and ninth (major) in the last movement of Grieg's piano concerto.

(2) *The Diminished Triad on the Dominant (with the possible addition of a Minor Seventh)*

The chord with the seventh appears with great effect in the slow movement of Dvořák's fourth symphony.

(3) *The Diminished Triad (and Seventh) on the Dominant in the Minor Key*

The first bars of Debussy's quartet show this chord used with the seventh added.

THE MAJOR COMMON CHORD ON THE SHARPENED FOURTH DEGREE

This chord, as a chromatic harmony, makes rare appearances and must be accepted with reservation. All three notes are chromatic. It is therefore a chord very remote from the diatonic key. A well-known example from Dvorak's *New World* symphony will show a very effective use.

Most of the chords discussed in this chapter belong in practice to the realm of actual composition rather than to students' harmony exercises. It must also be recognized that only those chords which have become an accepted part of harmonic technique in general have been considered; it is of course possible to foresee the extension of chromatic harmony to cover all (non-diatonic) triads and sevenths on every diatonic and chromatic degree of the scale.

The average student will find these chords edged tools, and, unless he has an unusually developed harmonic sense, will almost certainly be guilty of many crude pieces of harmony if he tries to use them indiscriminately. It is nevertheless important that he should make himself well acquainted with the possibilities which they hold. The chords shown in this chapter will provide enough material for experiment to last him a long time.

It may be helpful to include here some of the advice generally offered in dealing with such chords. Three factors seem, to some extent, to govern the effective use of chromatic harmonies in general.

1. Root relationships. Chords with roots a semitone, or a minor or major third apart, can generally follow each other with good effect.

2. The presence of at least one note common to both chords in the progression.

Ex 156.

C major.

3. What Bairstow calls a 'link' chord. In other words a chord either diatonic or chromatic which can serve as a bridge between the tonality of the passage and the momentary tonality of the chromatic chord employed.

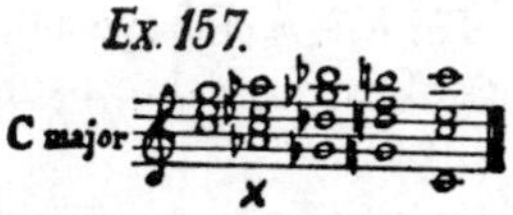

At least one of these factors is almost always present in progressions to and from these chromatic chords.

In extended chromatic passages either a stationary note common to all the chords, or some definite scale passage (diatonic or chromatic) will help to bind the harmony into coherence. These need not necessarily be in the bass.

A short passage near the end of the Dvořák 'cello concerto already quoted in this chapter shows the use of the single note, here in the top part, binding two very chromatic chords into a coherent harmonic structure in B major.

An example of a scale passage in whole tones unifying a series of very remote chromatic harmonies may be quoted from Vaughan Williams's *On Wenlock Edge*. None of the remoteness inherent in this kind of harmonic procedure is lost by this unification; in fact it makes the impression far more forceful.

A passage from Elgar's *The Kingdom* shows a three-note scale movement in the bass binding a series of extreme chromaticisms.

Chapter Nine

CHROMATIC HARMONY IN THE DIATONIC SCALE SYSTEM

What composers seek to-day is freedom from the limits of the major and minor scale-system. . . . A composer [in the sixteenth century] writing for instance in the scale or mode of G, had two thirds at his command, two sixths, and two sevenths. . . . He could even use the two forms simultaneously in two different parts; the English composers were constantly doing so. A modern composer has only to develop this method of proceeding to obtain the full freedom of a twelve-note scale, with no need of becoming either arbitrary or chaotic. It can thus be realized that music in 1600 did indeed stand at the crossroads, but saw only one arm. That was right at the time, but now the hour has come to go back and see where the other arm points us. R. O. MORRIS (*Polyphony*; Grove).

THIS chapter is frankly speculative, and claims to be no more than a personal point of view. It is nevertheless the primary justification for the treatment of chromatic harmony in this book, and the hypotheses to be set forth were indeed the main incentive to the particular approach to the subject.

The quotation from R. O. Morris's excellent article on *Polyphony* in the fourth edition of Grove's dictionary gives food for much thought. The direction which these thoughts have taken in this chapter must not be debited to Dr. Morris's account.

The position in 1600 was briefly this. Harmonic sense had been developing gradually during the polyphonic period. Men's minds had become accustomed to the harmonic implications of the intervals between the several simultaneous rhythmic strands which made up the musical texture, and these harmonic implications had become to some extent fixed and accepted. The normal cadential formulae show the clearest and earliest examples of this process.

The chief cause of this development of a harmonic sense lay in the fact that 'to attend to two melodies simultaneously requires intense concentration; to attend to three is beyond even the most expert capacity, so far as the writer, searching carefully, has been able to discover.' (R. O. Morris, ibid.) As the number of voices increased in the polyphonic period the synthesis of the intervals was the real impression conveyed to the hearer; in fact a vertical (harmonic) rather than a horizontal (melodic) experience. Theoretically sixteenth-century technique was horizontal, or contrapuntal, but by 1600 there is no doubt that counterpoint was quite firmly founded upon a harmonic basis. Harmony was the inevitable result of contrapuntal evolution, because of the limitations of man's mental capacity, and the fact must be faced that after more than three hundred years the position is unaltered and a definite harmonic basis is still essential for the satisfactory realization of counterpoint in more than two parts.

By 1600 the modal system in the strict sense had, for practical purposes, almost ceased to exist. Transposition, extension of compass, and the merging of the Authentic and Plagal forms had been in part responsible; the constant employment of 'musica ficta' had finished the work. This last factor had robbed most of the modes of their individuality. In the second half of the sixteenth century the only mode retaining its real character was the Phrygian. This mode did not survive long, owing perhaps to its impracticability from a harmonic point of view (for example, the normal full close is not available in it).

The major and minor scale systems, much as we know them, had to a great extent superseded the modal system by 1600, though modal influences persisted and 'musica ficta' remained for long, possibly in reality until to-day. The adoption of these scale systems was the inevitable consequence of the growth of harmonic sense, for definite chordal relationships presuppose a scale system of a fixed series of intervals. The harmonic relationships such as those of chords on the tonic, dominant and subdominant easily led to key relationships of a similar order. This only became possible with the adoption of the major-minor key system, in which a definite interval series was present. The key relationship of dominant and tonic, for instance, would only be satisfactory if the two scales were compatible; in the modal system the contrast between the series starting on A (Æolian Mode) and that starting on E (Phrygian) would be nothing more than a contrast of modes each with a totally different and incompatible interval series; moreover the whole series of chord relationship in the two modes would be different. In the major-minor key system the scales of A (major or minor) and E (major or minor) are like and therefore comparable entities. Furthermore the modern major and minor modes have enough in common to permit satisfactory contrast between the two.

The evolution of key sense had progressed a long way before 1600. Byrd, for instance, in works like *Laudibus in sanctis* and the *Great Service* shows quite plainly that he was well aware of the possibilities of real modulation, that is to say, a definite shift of key centre. In earlier times 'modulation' had meant no more than cadential variation of a transitory nature (see Chapter XII).

The development of these fundamental chord and key relationships which presupposed a fixed major and minor scale system was the road down which one of the signposts of 1600 pointed, and along which music travelled for three hundred years or so. The emotional and structural possibilities opened up were vast, but the very fixing of chord, key, and interval relationships necessarily imposed restrictions in some directions where before there were none. The resources of a major and minor scale system with inherent and strongly felt tendencies of harmonic progression are necessarily limited compared with modal contrapuntal freedom.

The possibilities of real modulation with its emotional and structural implications, were complete gain; but constantly shifting key centres were not a satisfactory answer, when it came to matters of design, to the problems inevitably raised by the restrictions the system imposed within the key.

Composers from the time of Bach onwards seem to have been subconsciously aware of what had been lost in the change over to the fixed scale. This awareness takes shape in the form of the interpolation of notes and, later, chords foreign to the key employed within the compass of the key; in fact chromatic harmony without modulation. By this means the harmonic and melodic scope of the diatonic key system could be widened without losing the identity of the particular tonality in being at the time. Such chromatic interpolation could be momentary—a sudden splash of colour—or extended so far as to produce long passages of strange and seeming remoteness akin to journeys into uncharted regions. It could even lead to the simultaneous use of two or more contrasted keys without any suggestion of chaos.

An examination of some passages of a highly chromatic character seems to bear out these contentions.

First of all let us consider the scale envisaged by Morris in the quotation (Example 161a), and see how the three available optional notes outside the diatonic major scale could be used with the aid of accepted classical chromatic harmony.

It will be seen from the second illustration below (Example 161b) that the three optional notes can be harmonized in a variety of ways. (The scale has been transposed to E♭ for easy comparison with the next illustration.) This, of course, does not invalidate the latter part of the quotation from Morris. The use classical composers made of these extra notes was far other and more restricted than the use which Morris suggests. It does, however, show that some of the possibilities of these chromatic notes were realized in classical times.

The next illustration, the last line of the *Little Organ Book* version of 'O Mensch, bewein' shows all three optional notes under discussion and four of the possible chromatic harmonies, used by Bach within the space of two bars. The key centre throughout the passage remains E♭ major (despite the chromatic sequence).

The result of Bach's harmonization of the passage is one of the most moving things in music.

Good examples of the remote kind of tonality made possible by chromatic harmony are to be found in the 'Chaos' representation in Haydn's *Creation*. Both the passages quoted can easily be analysed with-

out reference to modulation. The whole movement achieves a remarkable atmosphere of vagueness and unreality. Haydn has chosen to represent chaos within the framework of classical chromatic harmony, but it may be said fairly that in doing this he has, without going outside the key centre of C minor in either of the examples in Ex. 162, widened the tonality very greatly.

Notes on the harmony

A. (1) Dominant minor ninth. (2) Tonic chromatic ninth. (3) Supertonic chromatic ninth. (4) ? Dominant harmony (B♮ understood). (5) German sixth on flat supertonic. (6) Dominant seventh. (7) Tonic. (8) Neapolitan sixth. (9) Supertonic chromatic ninth.

B. (1) Augmented sixth on (flat) submediant (see page 56). (2) Dominant minor ninth. (3) German sixth on (flat) submediant. (4) Dominant seventh.

A Mozart example of an extended piece of chromatic harmony without any real modulation shows how all twelve notes of the chromatic scale could be used within the compass of the key harmonically. Mozart was very fond of these long drifts of chromatic harmony, and the resulting vagueness of tonality. The passage repays close study.

Ic
German 6th on ♭VI
Allegro & andante (K.188) Mozart
Ic
V
I
Ex.164. Allegro.
5th Symphony. Beethoven.
pizz.
C minor.
ppp
pizz.
arco col 8va
V
VI
sempre pp
Ic
VI
Ic
V.
I.

The famous passage at the end of the scherzo of Beethoven's fifth symphony is a splendid instance of the mysterious effect produced by chromatic harmony. Of course many factors go to the making of this very wonderful section, but it may be fairly claimed that the use of the French sixth on the submediant and the supertonic chromatic ninth has much to do with the remoteness achieved. From a technical point of view the double pedal C (inverted) is worthy of notice. (Ex. 164).

Brahms carries the process of enlarging the scope of the diatonic scale a stage further. By employing chromatic harmony within the limits of classical usage, he succeeds in evolving something like a double tonality; a pointer to the efforts at polytonality which have proved so problematic in later times.

His use of the minor chord on the subdominant in the major key has already been referred to in the chapter on that chord. An examination of a passage from the *Handel Variations* will show how he superimposed one tonality upon another without losing the essential key sense of the main key.

Here the use of the minor chord on IV and the dominant minor ninth, which, it must be remembered, is a chromatic chord in the major keys, gives rise to a mixed tonality of B♭ and E♭ minor throughout the passage.

An even more striking example of this dual tonality is found in the opening of the slow movement of Brahms's fourth symphony. Here again the minor chord on IV, the dominant minor ninth and in addition a strong hint of the major chord on the flattened VI and minor dominant chord, superimpose a strong A minor feeling on the key of E major, which remains the real key throughout.

In the opening of his fifth symphony Vaughan Williams shows quite clearly how the freedom of two tonalities can be achieved without any break away from the main stream of musical evolution. In the lovely passage, the opening of which is quoted below, the tonalities of C major and G major are naturally and inevitably blended.

There is no difficulty in explaining this passage within the scope of classical chromatic harmony. It is merely, as has been shown earlier, a case of supertonic chromatic harmony resolving on the tonic in C major.

It was shown in the end of the previous chapter (VIII) how almost complete chromatic freedom in harmony within the key could be attained by means of some simple linking device, such as a sustained note or scale passage in some prominent part. The elimination of such a link is the next step towards complete chromatic freedom. An example from *The Kingdom* shows one method of progress along this road, by reducing the link to a minimum.

The development of chromatic harmony in its most important aspect has had the effect of widening the harmonic scope of the diatonic scale system within the key. It has given back to composers something of the freedom which was lost when the modal system was abandoned. It has, in its logical and natural development, given the chance of almost complete chromatic freedom within the key, and some measure of polytonality.

This development has necessarily come about harmonically, even though the origin of most chromatic harmony has been the chromatic passing note.

Armed with the chromatic freedom which three hundred years of harmonic evolution has achieved, composers might well turn again to the sixteenth century and investigate the path of melodic and contrapuntal freedom to which Dr. Morris points, and along which men like Vaughan Williams and Sibelius have already travelled some considerable way. It seems that here lies the way to complete freedom without either revolution or chaos.

Chapter Ten

MODULATION

CHROMATIC PIVOT CHORDS

MODULATION is really a problem of structure. The mechanical process involved in passing from one key to another (and that is usually all that is taught, as students know to their cost when they begin to try their hands at actual composition), is a relatively simple matter. The ability to 'modulate from key X to key Y in four chords by means of a pivot-chord chromatic in the first key and diatonic in the second' may be laudable, but is of little practical or musical use unless key relationships and key structure are thoroughly understood.

It will probably be best to deal with the mechanical processes first of all.

Modulation may be defined as the art of moving from one key to another in a logical and inevitable way. It may involve a complete and prolonged shift of key centre, or may imply only a transitory change of key. In each case the words logical and inevitable in the definition are the crux of the matter.

The most important means of effecting modulation is by the 'pivot chord' method. The pivot chord is a chord common to both keys involved. It may be diatonic in both keys, diatonic in one and chromatic in the other, chromatic in both, or used in any of these chromatic ways with an enharmonic change involved.

The first of these types of pivot chord has been dealt with in the first volume of *The Oxford Harmony*. The other types which may be classed together under the heading 'Chromatic modulation' must now be examined. If the student has followed the description of the uses of the main chromatic chords in Chapters I to VIII he should know how to approach and quit these chords. He is therefore in a position to deal with them from the mechanical point of view whether they are approached or quitted as chromatic chords in their 'pivot' function.

It is proposed to consider each of the more usual chromatic chords in turn and show how it can be used for purposes of modulation.

One further definition is necessary. A key is said to be established when the dominant to tonic progression in it has been heard. Neither of the chords involved need necessarily be in root position. It is not suggested that this ruling is the whole truth or even nothing but the truth, but for the moment it may suffice as a general principle.

SUPERTONIC CHROMATIC CHORDS

The supertonic chromatic triad and even more the supertonic chromatic discords have, as already pointed out, a strong tendency to suggest modulation to the dominant key, being in fact dominant chords of the dominant key. This use (Example 168, A1) and the process in reverse (B1), (the dominant chord in the first key becoming the supertonic chromatic chord in the second) are a commonplace of music from the Bach–Handel period onwards. Strictly speaking it is doubtful if the term 'Chromatic modulation' should be applied to the first of these cases (A1). The keys involved are so nearly related that the modulation can usually be explained on purely diatonic grounds, taking some ordinary diatonic chord common to both keys as the pivot, and the 'supertonic chromatic' chord as the real dominant of the new key.[1]

The skeleton harmony of the process showing *one* approach and resolution is given below. In A1 the pivot chord is chromatic in the existing key, and diatonic in the new key; in B1 it is diatonic in the existing key and chromatic in the new key.

A few musical examples will show the normal uses.

[1] The second case (Ex. 168 B1) can also be explained as a purely diatonic modulation looking upon the first chord as the real pivot (i.e. dominant of F), and the

A final quotation shows the complete return journey via B1 and A1.

The other theoretical possibilities of the supertonic chromatic triad (or discord) as a pivot chord chromatic in one key and diatonic in the other, may be summarized as follows.[1]

second as a supertonic chromatic chord in F, resolving normally. This explanation is rather far-fetched. An alternative theory is to regard the third chord as a tonic chromatic seventh in C, becoming the dominant seventh of F.

As always, the musical effect must be the final deciding factor, and in the end there is little doubt that such progressions as A1 and B1 generally *sound* like modulations by supertonic chromatic pivots.

[1] Bare harmony and only one approach and resolution given. This method will be followed throughout this section.

Ex 172

A. *Chromatic in the first key, diatonic in the second.*

B. *Diatonic in the first key, chromatic in the second.*

Of these only two (A2 and B3) seem to take their place with any regularity in actual music. A few words may be said about the rest. A3 is essentially unsatisfactory, as the pivot chord is the tonic of the new key, and it is almost impossible to make this sound convincing. A similar situation may be seen in the case of modulations by ♭II, but here the key relationship of C and D♭ is, for reasons which will be discussed later, more convincing than that of C and D. A4 in which the supertonic chromatic chord becomes the submediant chord of the MINOR key an augmented fourth higher, is a crude and unmusical way of introducing this modulation. It is hard to think of any way of making it satisfactory. B2 is equally jerky and unpromising. B4, though an extreme modulation, seems to hold out the most promise of success.

To return to the two commonly used modulations in this group, A2 is very often found in Bach, especially in going to a minor key. The seventh can, of course, be added only when the destination is a minor key. The following beautiful examples show Bach's use of the formula.

Ex. 173. 'Vater unser' Bach

B3 is quite a useful modulation to a key a tone below the prevailing key. The tonic chord of the first (major) key becomes the supertonic chromatic chord of the new key.

The possibilities of using the chord as a pivot, chromatic in both keys, may be summed up thus:

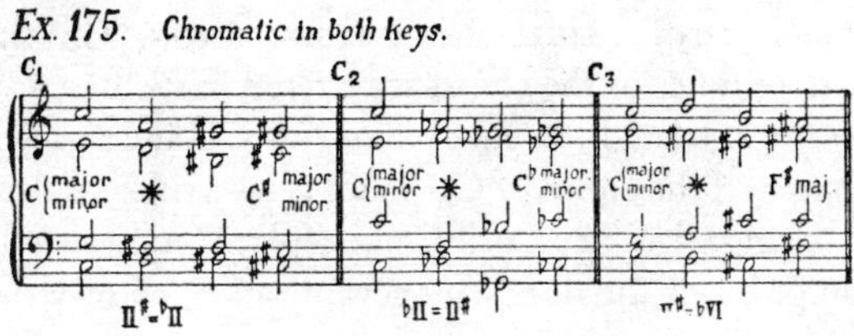

Examples of the highly chromatic modulations C1 and C2 are given in the section concerned with modulation by means of the flat supertonic chord (p. 108).

C3 produces the same difficulties as A4, of which it is, of course, only a technical variant.

C4 is again only a technical variant of B4, but it seems less promising.

C5 in which the supertonic chromatic seventh becomes the tonic chromatic seventh of the new key, again suffers partly from the same disadvantages as A3; furthermore, the difficulty of quitting the tonic chromatic chord convincingly in the new key makes it of little use.

C6, the reverse process of C5, is, on the other hand, a really effective modulation. The reason may be that the tonic chromatic seventh is easy to approach in its own key, and thus approached sounds quite natural and convincing, but it is difficult to follow it up as a real chromatic chord without modulation.

The supertonic chromatic seventh may be used as a pivot chord in what is generally termed ENHARMONIC MODULATION. This simply means that one or more notes of the chord are altered in spelling *and character* to form a new chord, though, in equal temperament at any rate, the sounds remain unaltered. If the chord of C♯ major is re-written as that of D♭, no enharmonic change has necessarily taken place; it is merely a case of altered spelling: but if the dominant seventh of C be re-written with an

E♯ replacing the F, though the sound remains the same in equal temperament, the character of the note and of the chord has changed. The matter of spelling in these enharmonic changes is purely arbitrary in most instrumental writing, and composers generally adopt the spelling which is easiest for the performer to read, however much it may obscure the harmonic propriety of the passage.

If the seventh of the supertonic chromatic chord is enharmonically changed, the chord becomes an augmented sixth of the German breed in another key. The possibilities are limited to two outward, and two return journeys. Reduced to their barest form they are:

D1 is a striking and useful modulation in a chromatic context. An Elgar example shows the pivot chord in its second inversion, well camouflaged with unessential notes and a suspension.

D2 is a rather jerky process. A Chopin example in which plenty of time is allowed for the chords to take effect (even though there is more than a suggestion of an extraneous but fleeting modulation to G on the way) seems to be the most satisfactory kind of treatment available.

D3 is really akin to II♯—♭II (see Example 194). In this form it suffers from the difficulty of making the resolution of the augmented sixth on the flat supertonic convincing in the new key and not merely a half close.

D4 is a rarely found modulation. Like D3 it is very nearly related to ♭II—II♯. Example 193 can equally well be explained as a case of this process if the harmony of bar 3 is regarded as the real pivot chord and bar 2 as ♭II in the original key.

THE MAJOR CHORD ON THE FLAT SUPERTONIC

This chord and its more common first inversion (the Neapolitan sixth) provide most useful pivots. When approached as chromatic harmonies they lead easily to keys on the flat side. The reverse process leads equally naturally to the sharp side. The possibilities of their use as chromatic in both keys are vague, except in the cases cited below.

The mechanical process involved may be briefly set out as follows:

Ex. 181.

B. *Diatonic in the first key: chromatic in the second.*

Ex. 182.

C *Chromatic in both keys.*

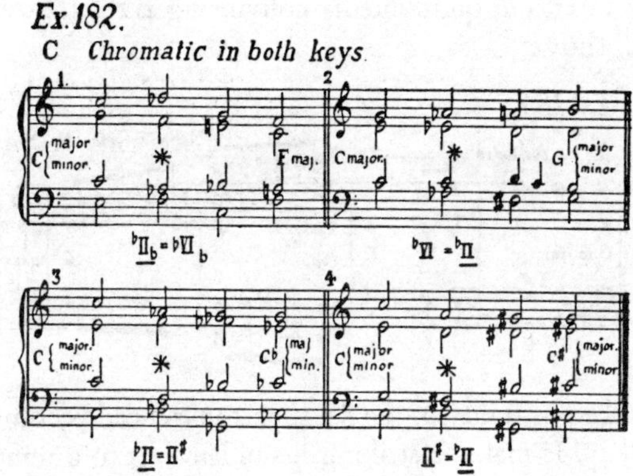

In practice, A1 in which the chord on the flat supertonic becomes the subdominant chord of the new key, is a natural and easy way of getting to a key a major third below the existing key. It is quite frequently found in Beethoven and Schubert, and is a generally accepted chromatic pivot.

A2 in which the flat supertonic becomes the dominant chord of the new key (often getting a minor seventh added in the course of its functioning as a pivot) is rarer, but undoubtedly convincing as the following Brahms example will show.

A3 shows the possibility of the flat supertonic chord becoming the tonic of the new key. It makes a striking if sudden shift to a remote key, and needs very careful handling to be made convincing.

In A4, the only other really useful change in this section, the chord becomes the submediant of the new key (MINOR only).

The return journey, in which the pivot chord is the flat supertonic in the new key and diatonic in the first key (B1–4) is on the whole more usual.

B1 where the pivot is the subdominant chord in the original key is a satisfactory way of modulating to a key a major third above.

B2 in which the dominant of the first key becomes the flat supertonic of the second, leading to an 'extreme' key an augmented fourth higher,

is rarely found, but is nevertheless a very striking modulation. It is, for some reason, more difficult to make musical than A2, which actually achieves the same result. (Ex. 189).

B3 is however one of the commonest ways of modulating to a key a semitone below the original one in the classical and romantic periods. The tonic chord of the first key becomes ♭II in the second.

In B4 the submediant chord in the *minor* key becomes the flat supertonic in the new key (dominant major or minor). This is a well-established use from the time of Bach onwards. (Ex. 191).

A few cases in which the pivot chord is chromatic in both keys are important. C1 only differs from A4 in the small technical detail that the flat submediant chord is chromatic in the major key. Since it has normally to be followed by a dominant harmony of the new key, which is common to both major and minor mode, the difference is of little more than mere academic importance, but somehow the result is less satisfactory, and in practice it is rarely used.

C2, the reverse of C1, is much more satisfactory. Here the chord on the

Ex. 191.
B4
a. Slow.
Matthew Passion 74. Bach.
F minor.
C minor
B4
Molto allegro.
Str. Quartet K. 387. Mozart.
b.
F minor.
C minor
Ex. 192.
C2. Allegretto vivace.
a
E♭ major.
cresc.
String Quartet Op. 59. No 1. (2). Beethoven.
f p
B♭ maj.
C2.
b. Brünnhilde.
Sagst du mir was du willst; wer bin ich, wär' ich dein Wil - le nicht?
A maj. pp
(on a pedal point)
'Walküre' II. 2. Wagner.
pp
p dolce.
più p
E major

♭VI in the already established major key is a very definite and striking chromatic harmony, and its change to the chord on ♭II is a really useful way of modulating to the dominant. (Ex. 192).

C3 and C4 are difficult and highly chromatic modulations in which the flat supertonic chord becomes the supertonic chromatic chord and vice versa. The remoteness of the key change involved generally calls for change of notation. This is not the same thing as enharmonic modulation in which at least one note of a chord alters not only its name but also its character. It is merely a matter of spelling.

TONIC CHROMATIC CHORDS

The tonic minor triad in the major key, and the tonic major triad in the minor key are of no particular interest in real chromatic modulation. The change from major to minor or minor to major of the tonic chord constitutes in itself a change of mode, and any modulation following this can generally be explained as diatonic.

The tonic chromatic seventh on the other hand is one of the most frequently used pivots in chromatic modulation when approached as a chromatic chord in the first key. As has already been pointed out, quitting this chord as a real chromatic harmony in the new key is a difficult and often unsatisfactory process. It follows that a pivot chord which becomes the tonic seventh of the new key will be comparatively rare in use.

The theoretical possibilities of the tonic seventh as a pivot chord in chromatic modulation may be reduced to these:

A1, which is, in reality, little more than a diatonic modulation, is probably the commonest modulation in all music from the time of Bach onwards. One beautifully balanced and timed instance from Beethoven will suffice to show the process.

A2 on the contrary, is practically useless, for the reason already given. It is furthermore unbelievably clumsy, and though cases of its use no doubt exist it is hard to see how it could be made effective and musical.

B1 and B2, in which the tonic seventh becomes the supertonic chromatic seventh and the reverse process, have already been considered in the section dealing with the supertonic chromatic chords in modulation on page 100.

It now remains to deal with the enharmonic possibilities of the chord. C1 is an effective and beautiful way of modulating to a key a major third higher. It is probably the most used enharmonic modulation in music. (Ex. 199).

C2. The return journey is less satisfactory and rarely found. A Schubert example shows one way of accomplishing the feat by resolving the tonic seventh on a supertonic chromatic ninth in the new key.

The remaining cases, in which the augmented sixth on the flat supertonic is involved, are extremely difficult because of the dual personality of that chord (see Chapter VI). Two fairly definite examples of C3 are given below. C4 has again the added difficulty of quitting the tonic seventh in the new key and seems almost hopelessly improbable.

THE MAJOR CHORD ON THE FLATTENED SUBMEDIANT IN THE MAJOR KEYS

The chief theoretical possibilities of ♭VI in modulation are these:

All the outward modulations in section A are possible and effective. A1 is an extreme key-change, and the Schubert smash-and-grab type of procedure is very striking.

A2 is less common. The following Brahms example is completely satisfying, if leisurely by comparison with Schubert's youthful enthusiasm for getting straight to the new key.

A3 is really more of a transition than a modulation. It is in fact almost a direct jump into the new key. It is a delightful and very favourite device

of all composers from Haydn onwards. Three typical examples show how it was used. The Tschaikovsky quotation shows the outward and return journeys. Many instances can be found in Sibelius (e.g. the second symphony) which seems to suggest that the process is by no means dead yet.

Little need be said of the return journeys (B1, 2 and 3). B1 and 2 are only technically chromatic modulations, depending solely on the 'tierce

de Picardie' in the final chord for this classification. B3 sounds more definitely chromatic, so a few examples may be quoted. It is a very common practice, especially in Schubert. (Ex. 206).

The cases in group C have already been dealt with as far as they are of practical value, C1 and 2 on page 100, C3 and 4 on page 106.

CHORDS OF THE AUGMENTED SIXTH ON THE FLATTENED SUBMEDIANT (♭VI♯6)

The theoretical possibilities of these chords in modulation are given below in crude form.

A1 and A2 show the augmented sixths on the flattened second and sixth degrees changing places. All three nationalities of the chord are, in theory at any rate, available. In practice the explanation of these modulations as strictly chromatic is somewhat doubtful. It is at least equally convincing to regard the first chord of A1 as the real pivot, in which case the augmented sixth becomes merely ♭II♯6 in G. There is also the difficulty in deciding to which key the augmented sixth really belongs, as has already been pointed out in earlier chapters.

Some fairly clear examples are given below:

In both these examples the German form of the augmented sixth is used. A clear-cut instance of the French form is well seen in a Chopin *Polonaise*.

The return journey seems to be less often used. The issue is less clear as the normal resolution of the flat supertonic augmented sixth is upon the tonic which, if the augmented chord is regarded as the pivot, has to shed its identity as the tonic of the first key and become the dominant of the second. Two examples are given below. It is left to the reader to bring in a verdict upon them. The first shows a German sixth over a pedal; the second a French sixth.

A much more subtle method of modulating by means of an enharmonic change of the French sixth has been touched upon on page 65. It is possibly more common than is generally supposed and certainly sounds logical and musical despite its theoretical complications.

In B1 the augmented sixth on the flattened submediant becomes the dominant seventh of the key a semitone above by enharmonic change of the sixth. The German form of the chord is the only one officially recognized, though it is also possible to use the Italian form by the simple expedient of leaving out the fifth, and even the French form occasionally makes a somewhat surprising if belated appearance. This applies to the whole section B of these modulations.

B1 is an extremely striking modulation, though rare. Two memorable examples are quoted.

B2 in which the dominant seventh becomes the augmented sixth on the flattened submediant (the reverse of B1) is one of the commonest and most successful of enharmonic modulations. Schubert was obviously fond of it, and Brahms produces strings of modulations made in this way, as the third example quoted below shows.

B3 and 4 are dealt with on page 111. B5 and 6 on page 102.

THE AUGMENTED SIXTH ON THE FLATTENED SUPERTONIC

It has already been shown how difficult it is to pin down this chord to any one specific key. The theoretical possibilities are easy enough to see.

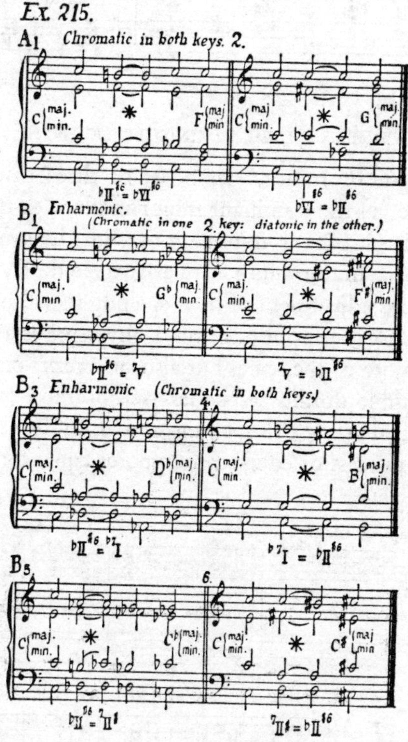

A1 and A2 have already been considered on page 115. B3 and 4 on page 111. B5 and 6 on page 102. It remains to consider cases B1 and B2. B1 produces a beautiful change to a remote key. An example from a Chopin *Nocturne* in which the chord appears in its last inversion shows how easy and natural this change can be.

Another passage from an early Chopin work illustrates the enharmonic change of the dominant seventh to the augmented sixth on the flat supertonic.

CHORDS OF THE DIMINISHED SEVENTH

Every key, major or minor, can boast of three distinct diminished sevenths. They are (1) the dominant minor ninth with the root omitted; (2) The supertonic chromatic minor ninth with the same omission; (3) the tonic chromatic minor ninth similarly treated. By inverting these chords and judicious adjustment of their spelling it will be found that one or other of these chords in root position or inversion is available not only on each diatonic note of the scale, but also on every chromatic note. In fact the three possible diminished series are common to all keys by the simple process of altering the spelling and possibly some enharmonic adjustment. This process of course presupposes equal temperament.

The following table will show how any diminished seventh can belong to any key major or minor by enharmonic change.

1. G (dominant); C (supertonic chromatic); D (tonic chromatic).
2. B♭ (dominant); E♭ (supertonic chromatic); F (tonic chromatic).

3. E (dominant); A (supertonic chromatic); B (tonic chromatic).
4. C♯ (dominant); F♯ (supertonic chromatic); G♯ (tonic chromatic).

It will be seen that it is theoretically possible to modulate to any key by using the diminished seventh as a chromatic or enharmonically changed pivot chord.

It would be absurd to attempt to give illustrations of all these possible changes. Two types of modulation by this method stand out; the normal carefully balanced and timed pivot modulation, and the vague tonality type of passage in which many keys are hinted at without being definitely established. One outstanding example of each must suffice here.

The Beethoven passage shows a beautifully smooth enharmonic change with plenty of time for its full implications to be felt. The remarkable ending of Bach's *Chromatic Fantasia* is a good example of transitions to various keys by means of the diminished seventh. This whole work should be studied in detail. A close examination of its uses of the chord will reveal almost all the possibilities.

Although the diminished seventh seems to be a heaven-sent gift to the hard-pressed examination candidate faced with some intricate problem of modulation, it is really a difficult chord to use with good effect. Its success depends upon a harmonic background of a distinctive chromatic kind, the kind typified by minor ninths.

VARIOUS CHROMATIC CHORDS

The remaining generally accepted chromatic chords must be discussed very briefly in modulation.

1. *The Diminished Triad on the Supertonic*

For purposes of modulation this chord generally assumes the character of an incomplete diminished seventh and is of some use in that form, but like other borrowings from the minor mode (with the exception of some of the possibilities of ♭VI) it is not of much importance as a real chromatic pivot chord.

2. *The Minor Triad on the Subdominant*

Another borrowing from the minor mode. The theoretical possibilities are these:

The outgoing cases A1–3 are very questionable as chromatic modulations. The minor subdominant chord if approached from the tonic implies in itself transitory modulation to some extent; the approach from the dominant is little better, as the dominant chord in these cases has a strong supertonic chromatic flavour in relation to the subdominant minor chord.

B1 and 3 are more satisfactory, though in reality only the 'tierce de Picardie' in the new key makes them 'chromatic modulations'. Schubert made considerable use of them. Many instances of B1 and B3 can be found in his works.

B2 (which sounds like a present-day attempt at what is for some inconceivable reason called in academic circles 'Modal Harmony') is much rarer. A rather debatable instance is given:

3. *The Major Triad (plus Seventh or Ninth) on the Major Submediant*

These chords are generally accepted as chromatic chords. A modulation or transition to a key a tone higher by this means (the submediant major chord becoming the dominant of the new key) is one of the most frequently used key changes in music from the time of Bach and Handel. The formula given below is almost a commonplace. It is one of the few chromatic modulations which can be found in almost every movement of most standard works. The formula works well in sequence; strings of such transitions are apt to occur in less inspired moments, though sometimes the result, especially in reverse (see the Schubert example of Example 228) is very telling.

Ex.226.
A.
B.
C major.
D major
minor.
C major
minor.
B♭ maj.

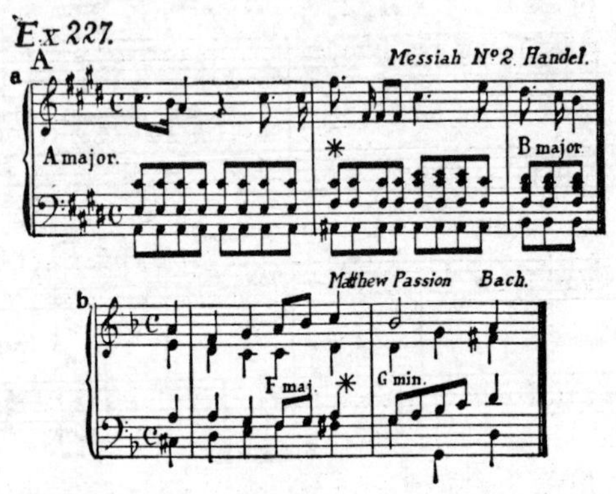
Ex 227.
A
a
Messiah Nº2. Handel.
A major.
B major.
Mathew Passion Bach.
b.
F maj.
G min.

c.
Presto.
G major.
A major
Symphony in D K.385 Mozart
B minor.
d.
Andante
K.453. Mozart.
E♭
F minor
Presto.
Quintet in C Schubert.
e.
C major.
D minor.
f.
Andantino.
Prelude 7. Chopin.
A major.
B min.

The reverse process B is equally available and adaptable to sequential treatment, as the following fine passage from Schubert's *Quartet-satz* shows.

It is very doubtful whether the other possibilities of the chord can be used satisfactorily in modulation (e.g., ^{7}VI♯ = ♭^{7}I : ^{7}VI♯ = ^{7}II♯ : ^{7}VI♯ = ♭VI♯^{6} : ^{7}VI♯ = ♭II♯^{6} : VI♯ = I or IV or ♭VI : or the reverse processes). It can safely be said that such remote methods of change must be very rare.

4. *The Major Triad and Seventh on the Flattened Mediant*

Some apparent instances of chromatic modulation by means of this chord (possibly plus its minor seventh) may be of interest if only to produce controversy. Of the following harmonic schemes 1 and 2 seem fairly authentic, 3 can be equally well explained as a perfectly normal diatonic modulation in which the real pivot chord is the first: C major (tonic) = subdominant of G major. 4 is really a key jump rather than a modulation.

1 is, in practice, quite useful as a Chopin example will show (Ex. 230 a).

An example of two modulations in quick succession by this means is seen in a well-known passage from *Gerontius* (Ex. 230 b).

2 brings with it the old difficulty of deciding whether the final chord, if major, is the tonic or the dominant of the new key. This is all too clearly seen in the fragmentary transition quoted from *Tristan.*

3 is quite a common formula, but is probably most easily explained as a simple diatonic modulation with either of the chords in bar 2 of the example given below regarded as the real pivot.

5. *The Major Triad and Seventh on the (Major) Mediant*

Passages like the following are frequently found.

It is easy to argue that the D major chord in the first bar is the real pivot and that the modulation is therefore diatonic (I=III), but the way the F♯ chord is emphasized and dwelt upon suggests that it is the pivot, and that in consequence this is a highly chromatic key change.

It will be obvious to the reader at this stage that in dealing with the more obscure and indefinite chromatic chords as pivots, the theoretical explanations and possibilities become more and more questionable, and much of what is said must necessarily be speculative. If these chromatic chords be admitted as suitable pivots for modulation the theoretical possibilities are almost inexhaustible, and explanations of them will become a matter of personal prejudice. In the end such explanations are of little importance. The musical effect is all that matters, and at this stage the student may well be left to experiment for himself. He may, for example, take this chord ^{7}III♯ and see how it might be used in various other ways, and then try to find examples in standard works. The value of such work lies in the fact that it will show the worthlessness of mere theoretical speculation, and the vital importance of what is real music. It will be quickly realized that such a common formula as the following, however plausible it may sound, has little musical worth; it belongs to the realm of the 'salon' at best, or the lowest type of popular dance music, or sentimental 'sacred solo'.

Ex. 234.

C major. * D

^{7}III♯ = ^{7}II♯

Enough has probably been said to show something of the methods and means of the mechanical and theoretical side of modulation by a pivot chord.

Chapter Eleven

OTHER MEANS OF KEY CHANGE

THEORISTS recognize two methods of effecting key change other than that of the pivot chord: (1) the pivot note process; (2) a clean-cut jump into the new key, with no connecting link whatever in the shape of pivot. (1) is generally acclaimed as a legal and proper way of achieving the desired end; (2) causes some embarrassment to most writers, who generally mention it and pass on to some other topic as quickly as possible.

Before discussing the claims of these methods and another method of perhaps equal importance, it is necessary to consider with some care the question of key relationships.

It was put forward as a hypothesis in Chapter IX that chordal relationships within a key or mode grew up as the result of the association of certain frequently used progressions of several melodic-rhythmic strands of counterpoint; the dominant-tonic relationship at the cadence, for instance. Eventually by common use all the 'chords' available acquired a definite personal character in relation to the tonic (or final) of the key or mode. This in turn, with the inevitable evolution of the diatonic major and minor scale system, led to the establishment of the wider relationships of one diatonic key to another.

Whether we regard the evolution of chromatic harmony as a partially subconscious effort on the part of composers to regain the harmonic and melodic freedom made available by 'musica ficta' in the modes, and lost very largely in the adoption of a fixed major and minor diatonic system, or as the direct result of the growth of key relationships in the new system, it is but one step further to establish relationships between chromatic chords and diatonic chords within the key, and this leads quite naturally to a similar connexion between chromatic keys (keys whose tonic chords do not appear in the prevailing diatonic scale) and the established diatonic key.

Everyone who has studied elementary diatonic harmony will remember the rather mystifying conclusion to which he was probably driven early in that enterprise, that some chords followed each other quite naturally and easily, while others could not be made to sound right no matter how correct the part writing might be. To aid him in keeping clear of the less happy juxtapositions of plain diatonic chords, a set of maxims was probably provided: such statements as 'any two diatonic chords which have one note in common may follow each other with good effect,' 'chords with roots a fourth or fifth apart nearly always produce a good harmonic progression'. These elementary rules, however unessential to the really musical student for his immediate purpose, are in actual fact the key to a far bigger subject; the whole basic problem of chord and key relationships.

It was pointed out in Chapter VIII that certain factors seemed to govern the effective use of all chromatic harmony, the two most important being the presence of a note in common, and root relationships. Professor Kitson went so far as to say, in dealing with chromatic chords, that 'any two chords may be used consecutively if they have at least one note in common', 'consecutive chords whose roots are a semitone apart are always good in effect'. (*The Evolution of Harmony*, p. 333.) To this may be added that chords with roots a major or minor third apart may be used in progression with equal success.

Two other factors were noticed in Chapter VIII in connexion with chromatic harmony. Firstly the link chord, of which more will be said later, and secondly the employment in extended chromatic passages of some scale passage (not necessarily in the bass) which had the effect of binding into logical coherence successions of even the most remote chords.

To a great extent these governing factors in the use of chromatic chords are equally operative in the case of chromatic modulation. Such a passage as the following is merely an extension of the use of a normal chromatic harmony.

It will be seen that certain chromatic key relationships are quite naturally established by these basic factors which seem to govern similar harmonic progressions. Though theoretically we may choose to look upon the first A♭ chord in the above example as a perfectly logical chromatic pivot, the key relationship is already established, and in such cases pivot chord or pivot note, though they may be there, are really unessential.

As we have already seen in the previous chapter, there are many cases of modulation to keys whose relationships are not thus established, and many ways of modulating to related keys, where the pivot chord is the essential factor in the process.

Turning to the theoretical system of key change by means of a *pivot note*, it will be found in nearly every case that the pivot note is nothing more than an adjunct to the pivot chord. A common note between a chromatic chord and the chord which follows or precedes it creates smoothness and does much to help the progression whether it involves modulation or not, but in most cases it is a secondary contingency. Parry, in his article in Grove, seems to take this view, when he says: 'These pivot-notes are, however, by no means indispensable. Modulations are really governed by the same laws which apply to any succession of harmonies whatsoever. . . .' It is very difficult to think of any case in standard works between 1600 and 1900 where a pivot note alone is responsible for a modulation. Its proper function is to give added coherence to a modulation whose key relationship is already established. A few examples will illustrate this.

Here the reiterated E acts as a pivot to the coming A major chord (the tonic of the new key). The possible key relationship is already there, and either the C major chord or the A major chord can be regarded as satisfactory pivot chords. The pivot note, however, is in this case the primary feature of the modulation, though not essentially the means by which it is achieved.

In Example 237 a similar process takes place, with the added point of interest that the pivot C alone represents the chord of A♭ and changes into the dominant note of the new key, F major.

A third example, from the *Siegfried Idyll* (Example 238), shows several good cases of the pivot note device. In all three instances marked A, B and C the key relationship is one which is normally considered as established (keys a third or fourth apart). In [A] the pivot note C is part of a chord common to both the keys concerned; the chord in question is the diminished fifth on the supertonic of E with a seventh added (= an added sixth on the subdominant minor of that key) which is also skeleton dominant major ninth in G. An interesting point is the omission of the pivot C in the sixth bar where the change is established; it is however very strongly felt. [B] is more important. The pivot note E♭ here is introduced alone; it may be regarded as a dominant minor ninth of G major (= supertonic chromatic of C major) and becomes momentarily a minor third in the new key C (major). [C] is an extension of this process; the pivot note A, the fifth of the dominant of G, is chromatically raised to A♯ (dominant augmented fifth) which undergoes an enharmonic change to a B♭; in this shape it becomes the dominant note of E♭.

The three quotations given above should convince the student of the very great artistic importance of the pivot note as a device in modulation, rather than as a means of effecting it in itself. The timing of the change of key outlook can be perfectly controlled by this means, and great music abounds in passages of tremendous significance in which this process is the outstanding feature.

There has always been much hesitation on the part of theorists over the question of key change without pivot chord or pivot note. Some call such changes, especially when they are of a temporary character, 'transitions' as opposed to real modulations. Parry points out that 'the two principles of pivot notes and the ambiguous pivot chords between them [*sic*] cover so much ground that it is not easy to find progressions in which either one or the other does not occur . . . (but) the frequency of their occurrence is not a proof of their being indispensable'. (Parry: *Modulation.* Grove's Dictionary, 4th Edition.)

We are not really concerned with the popular theory that some composers (Schubert is generally the favourite) were in the habit of going straight out of one key into another without any modulatory device whatever, but, such was their genius, with unfailingly good effect. Such examples as 186, 235, 236, 239, etc., might be cited as falling under this heading, but the writer has yet to see a case of this kind which lacks an already established key relationship if a definite pivot chord does not appear to be present. This is not in any way to condemn the direct jump type of modulation. It is a highly effective device used in combination with an established key progression.

When the key relationship is already there, the direct leap into the new key is both effective and common. The matter has already been touched upon; keys with tonics a semitone,[1] a minor third, or a major third above or below the original tonic have a close affinity; so obviously have the

[1] The relationship of keys a whole tone apart is less satisfactory. The reason may be that whereas the chord progressions from the tonic to a common chord on each of the other degrees mentioned are in themselves complete and satisfactory the progression I–II or I–II♯ sounds incomplete in itself and demands continuance by further progression.

subdominant and dominant. Modulation or transitory modulation to these keys is the direct counterpart of the effective use of their equivalent chords whether diatonic or chromatic. The device is often used sequentially in a series of transitory modulations. A few examples will make this clear:

1. A passage showing a direct jump to a key a semitone above (Neapolitan sixth relationship) partially sequential.

2. The reverse process; a sequential passage touching upon keys a semitone below each other.

3. Sequential direct modulation to keys a minor or major third above.

4. Direct jumps to keys a major or minor third below.

A 'bridge chord' or its possible extension into something like a transient modulation can be used as a link between two keys in much the same way as in chromatic harmony. It generally takes the form of a chord or progression representing a new (third) key, which new key acts as a link between the two principal keys involved in the modulation. The following characteristic passage from a Haydn quartet will show the process (Example 243). The modulation is from C minor to D major, a comparatively unrelated

key. The passage marked * —— * is a transitory modulation, or rather transition without real confirmation of the key which is little more than hinted at, to F♯ minor by means of an enharmonically changed (supertonic) diminished seventh; the F♯ minor chord is then treated as a diatonic chord (mediant) in D major and a perfectly straightforward diatonic modulation to D ensues. In this case it will be seen there is no really definite pivot chord between C minor and D major. (It would be straining theory rather far to regard the diminished seventh, quitted as it is, as belonging to D major; that is not the musical effect in performance.) It would be possible to think of the A as a pivot note, but this is a secondary point. The main device in this case is the bridge key.

A fragment from the *Meistersinger*, quoted by Parry as an example of modulation in which pivot chord and pivot note are both absent, seems to fall into this category. It is worth careful study, for though the key relationship is already present, F major to E minor, the means by which the change is brought about are unusual.

The passage begins in F major (there is just a possibility of its being considered in C to start with from the context, but the chord marked A seems to negative this) and modulates to E minor. Chord A is not an accepted chromatic harmony in E minor; chord B is equally improbable in F, but the relationship of chords A and B is simply the Neapolitan sixth relationship (i.e. chords with roots a semitone apart). If chord A is taken as the dominant of E♭ (IV in F equals V in E♭) that is, if it represents for the moment E♭, the whole process of the modulation becomes quite logical, chord B becoming ♭VI of E♭ with altered spelling equalling V of E minor.

Akin to this process of subsidiary key suggestion is the far simpler and much more common one which some theorists have called compound modulation. This really amounts to a series of transitory modulations in which several keys may be hinted at but not definitely established in the course of some more important and real shift of key centre. The subsidiary keys thus touched are kept well in the background, and passages of remote tonality and often of great effect may result. The usual method is that of a succession of pivot chords each of which takes, as it were, an unexpected turning and proceeds to a chord which, instead of establishing the expected new key, is in itself another pivot to further key change.

A very common example of this, much used in the Mozart-Haydn period, is a succession of 'dominant sevenths'.

Ex. 245.

Bach used the device frequently and at times with tremendous effect. The 'lightnings and thunders' chorus from the *Matthew Passion* is a good sample. The Alto Arioso 'Ah Golgotha' is a more subtle and most moving example in the same work.

The natural development of this use of transitions is the tightly packed modulatory passages in which transitions occur in quick succession between more important key changes. Parry quotes a good example from the *Hammerklavier* sonata. (Ex. 246).

Such passages, and they are of course of frequent occurrence in music of the eighteenth and nineteenth centuries, are analogous to the chromatic drifts already noticed in Chapters VIII and IX. As in the case of chromatic passages within the key, so in transitory modulations the same devices may be employed to give coherence to the process. One very notable device must be mentioned. The power of a scale passage, first of all in the bass, and at a later date in any part, to bind together extreme chromatic harmonies has been discussed. It is a like force in the modulatory counterpart, especially in the case of the chromatic scale. A well-known Wagner example will suffice to illustrate this. (Ex. 247).

The chief methods and devices of modulation have now been touched upon, and the student will be well advised to study for himself examples from standard works of all periods. Close analysis of modulations in actual music will teach him more about the subject than working innumerable mechanical exercises.

Ex. 246.
Adagio sostenuto.
(sotto)
E♭ major.
poco a poco due e poi tutte le corde.
f
una corda
f tutte le corde
una corda.
Pf. Sonata. Op. 106. Beethoven.
F♯ minor
Ex. 247.
A♭ major.
Walküre. Wagner.
E major

Chapter Twelve

MODULATION: HISTORICAL AND FORMAL ASPECTS

The historical aspect of modulation can well be taken with the problems of form and structure which are inseparable from the subject. It is proposed to make some attempt to deal very briefly with the two matters together.

It was stated at the beginning of Chapter X that modulation was really a problem of structure. It is equally true to say that form is a problem of key just as much as of subject matter, at least from the end of the sixteenth century to the end of the nineteenth.

In the modal period modulation as we understand it hardly existed at all. Real shift of key centre presupposed a fixed scale system which could only emerge as the modal system was transformed into the diatonic scale system. In modal times the phenomenon which looks to us like modulation was no more than the formation of cadences on various degrees of the mode which remained constant, in theory at any rate, throughout the work, or section of the work. Nevertheless these cadences were the starting-point from which the road led to the abandonment of the modal system in favour of the diatonic scale, the development of harmonic and key relationships, real shifts of key centre, and the organization of form and structure. Even in the modal period cadences were of great structural importance; not only did they bring to an end a musical sentence or paragraph, but they contained intrinsic emotional significance.

As the modal system gradually faded into the past, composers, particularly those of the English school, began to experiment with the possibilities of key. These experiments seem to fall into two main categories; one the use of something very near to our idea of transitory modulation for expressive purposes; the other the use of a shift of key centre for structural reasons, often without connecting modulation as we think of it.

The first of these cases can best be illustrated by one short quotation from Weelkes's *Gloria in excelsis*. Taken out of its context it looks like a rather

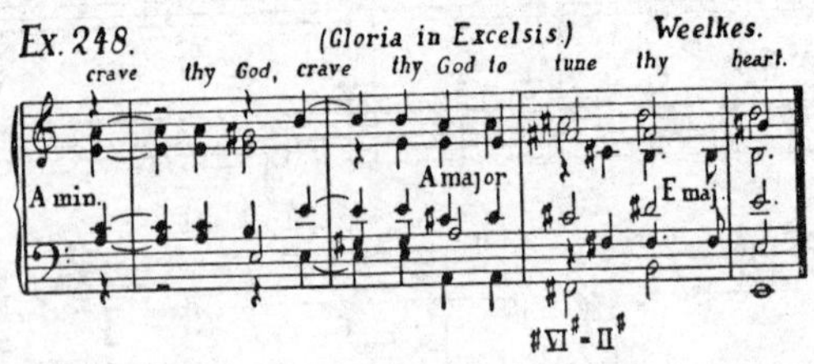

abrupt but perfectly logical modulation from A to E by means of the submediant major = supertonic chromatic pivot chord. It is in reality little more than a piece of graphic word painting, akin to the chromatic harmony and transient modulation of a later age. The modulation is momentary and normal tonality is almost immediately re-established, but the important point is that the ways and means of using key change for emotional or expressive purposes were in actual being even if the full significance of such a process was as yet undreamed of.

The other direction of experiment in which key contrast seems to make a tentative appearance is fairly common at the end of the period. A curious foretaste of it seems to occur in Tallis's *Lamentations*. The work as a whole is roughly in the Phrygian mode, but the section *Beth* (plorans ploravit) begins in what can only be described as the diatonic key of B♭ major. The previous section ends with a plagal cadence in the Dorian Mode; so the key relationship from a modern viewpoint is that of a major third below.

Ex. 219.

Something much more definite in the way of a real key scheme can be found in Byrd's work. A good case is the magnificent 'This day Christ was born' from *Psalms, Songs, and Sonnets*, 1611. Here real key planning seems to have taken place. The first section is in the key of G with an F♮ (Mixo-lydian); with the second section ('This day the just rejoice') comes a change of rhythm and a definite key shift to C major. The 'just' rejoice for some time in a lively manner, and then a complete change of mood takes place at the words 'saying, Glory be to God on High'; the time changes back to a dignified four-beat measure, and the key to A minor, and the whole passage is treated with great solemnity. In this section various related keys are touched in almost the manner of two centuries later, and a completely convincing return to the original key is made in the final section.

With the rise of instrumental music and the development of harmonic feeling in the seventeenth century, came the need of definite form. The old contrapuntal devices of imitative leads and the interweaving of rhythmic strands on which the structure of the polyphonic period was based had been for the time thrown overboard. In the case of instrumental music there were no words to give shape to the work. The problem of purely musical structure became a pressing one. Key sense was slowly developing, hampered by the absence of any really workable tempered scale. The period was one of transition, in which progress was bound to be slow. Parry sums up the situation well:

> Throughout the seventeenth century the system of keys was being gradually matured, but their range was extraordinarily limited, and the interchange of keys was still occasionally irregular (? occasional and irregular). Corelli, in the latter part of it, clearly felt the relative importance of different notes in a key and the harmonies which they represented, and balanced many instrumental movements on principles analogous to our own, though simpler; and the same may be said of Couperin, who was his junior by a few years; but it is apparent that they moved among accidentals with caution, and regarded what we call extreme keys as dangerous and almost unexplorable territory. (*Modulation*; Grove's Dictionary.)

By the Bach–Handel period the diatonic scale system and its harmonic implications had become firmly settled. Modulations to nearly related keys were understood and recognized; Bach's solution to the problems of tuning had thrown open the way to the extreme keys; yet with the exception of Bach himself composers seemed to be reluctant to explore the possibilities opened up. They were quite happy in their newly found mastery of the diatonic system, and content to use its simple chord relationships extensively without showing a burning desire to wander out into unexplored territories. Handel's great choruses, notably 'Hallelujah' from the *Messiah*, show what tremendous things could be accomplished within these limits—that is to say, almost wholly diatonic harmony with a very few transitions to closely related keys, and those not much more than temporary excursions returning quickly to the original key. Bach was a more adventurous spirit; he was less afraid of getting away from his main key for quite considerable stretches, and less hesitant about the distance travelled; the *Chromatic Fantasia* and the *G Minor Organ Fantasia* show how easily he could control and handle distant and extreme key changes. Yet even he, who had been so prodigal and daring in his use of almost every form of chromatic harmony, who had himself provided the ways and means for modulation to the most extreme keys, seemed reluctant to avail himself of the resources he had opened up, and for the most part contented himself with the limited and simple modulations which were the common property of composers of the time.

Perhaps the most profitable way of examining the relationship of form and modulation in this period is by analysing some 'suite' movements. In these it will be seen that the thematic material is generally little more than the elaboration and development of some figure or group of figures; it is really the key scheme which makes the structure of the movement. The following key analysis of a few such movements will illustrate how important the key scheme is.

First a perfectly straightforward Bach movement, the *Allemande* from the *French Suite in B Minor.*

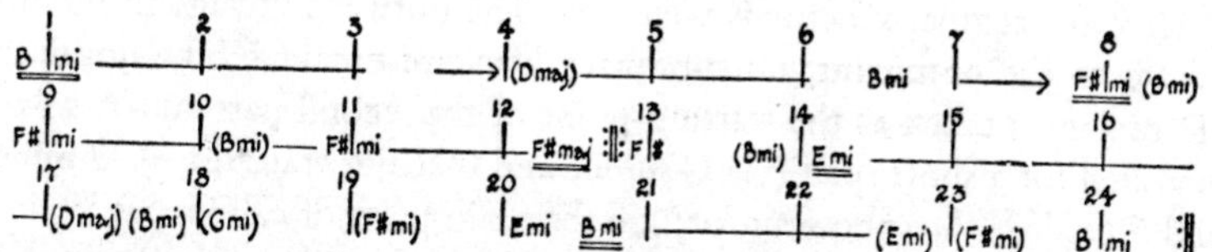

The important key centres are underlined. B minor holds the field for the first seven bars (with a transient glance at D major the relative major), then in bar 8 the dominant minor (F♯ minor) is established and is the new key centre, despite the two touches of B minor, till the double bar comes with its 'tierce de Picardie' (F♯ major) marking the end of the section. The second part takes the F♯ chord as a starting-point and then via B minor settles down into E minor (the subdominant minor) at bar 14. In bars 17 to 19 a series of transitions occurs returning to E minor. In bar 20 the return to the key of the movement is made (B minor), and that remains the key centre to the end with E minor and F♯ minor touched in bars 22 and 23. The real key centres are few and carefully spaced: B minor and F♯ minor in the first half; E minor and then B minor again in the second. The other key changes are completely subordinate and little more than chromatic harmonies in the existing key centre. The form of the key scheme might be roughly described as an outgoing journey to the sharp side and a return via the flat side (subdominant). This scheme is very common especially in movements in major keys.

An equally common scheme is well illustrated by the *Allemande* from Handel's *Suite in G Minor* (No. 2). Here the outward journey is to the relative major in the first part, and the sharp side is dealt with at the beginning of the second, the eventual return being again via the flat side (C minor).

1 Gmi — 2 — 3 — 4 → 5 Bb — 6 — 7 — 8 (Fmaj) — 9 Bb —
10 — 11 — :||: 12 Fmaj 13 → 14 Dmi — 15 — 16 — 17 (G mi) — 18 — Cmi
19 — 20 Bb 21 → 22 Gmi 23 — 24 — 25 — 26 (Cmi) — 27 Gmi — :||

Next a perfectly normal movement in a major key; the *Sarabande* from Bach's *French Suite in G.*

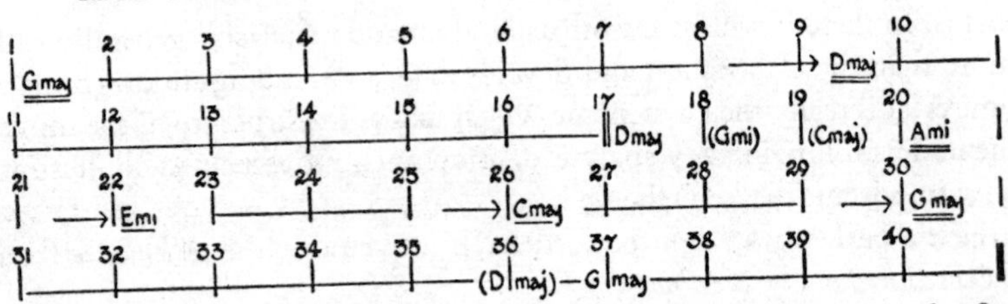

Here the regular scheme is well seen. The outward voyage in the first part is to the dominant; no subsidiary keys are touched. The dominant (D major) is taken as the starting-point of the second part and A minor is visited for a short spell (via G minor and C major transitions). E minor and C major (the subdominant) are the main ports of call in this section. The return to G major is made in bars 29 and 30 and that key retains its hold with only a transitory touch of D major till the end.

From these three examples it will be seen how, within the main plan of real shifts of key centre which form the structure, subsidiary transient modulations are used. It is obvious that they are either completely dependent upon the key centre in being at the time, and are not key changes in their own right, or that they are incidents in a real shift of key centre. The student should analyse many of the suite movements of the period; by so doing he will realize in the end that the form is in reality practically synonymous with the key scheme.

One general observation may be of use. The outward journey seems generally to be to the sharp side of the key of the movement, the return via the flat (subdominant) side. It may also be noted that a good deal of time seems to be devoted to establishing the tonic key both at the beginning and end of a movement.

The rise of sonata form in the eighteenth century shows even more clearly the vital importance of key scheme in the structure of music. The tonic-dominant (or in the minor keys the tonic-relative major) antithesis is the very foundation of the form.

The tonic-dominant antithesis should not be regarded as coming from the fugal subject-answer relationship, which was probably a legacy from the authentic and plagal modal usage rather than a definite key contrast. Its origin is almost certainly the process which has already been seen in the typical 'suite movement'. The minor-relative major antithesis was well founded in Tudor times, as in the 'Zion is wasted' section of Byrd's *Bow Thine Ear* and many madrigals; in fact the major-minor contrast is something which is fundamental in the diatonic key system.

The importance of the key contrast in early sonata form is proved by the fact that many cases exist in which the second subject is merely the first subject in the dominant key. In Haydn's symphony in D (No. 6 of the Salomon set) the first movement shows this well. Even in much later times, when the second subject developed into a highly organized section with strongly contrasted material, the key antithesis still seems to be the most important feature.

Parry, speaking of Haydn and Mozart, says: 'In the works of these two great composers we find at once the simplest and surest distribution of keys . . . each successive key which is important in the structure of the work is marked by forms both of melody and harmony, which, by the use of the most obvious indicators, state as clearly as possible the tonic to which the particular group of harmonies may be referred.' It is this very clarity in key definition which gives the unrivalled clarity of form to their work; it is equally the balance of key distribution that gives it the perfectly contrived proportion.

There are two matters of technical interest which must be considered at this point. The first is how to establish a new key centre. The mechanical means by which modulation can be made theoretically are relatively simple to manipulate. Transitory or subsidiary modulations in which the new key is little more than suggested are easily contrived, but the real shifting of the centre of tonality is a much more difficult matter. Marked insistence on the new dominant chord or the dominant-tonic cadence in the new key is one obvious way of making certain of the change.

Another method much used in the Mozart–Haydn period is the device of going one step beyond the key to which the modulation is being made and then as it were, coming down on it. This device is particularly useful in modulations to the sharp side; the process is to touch the dominant key of the new key. One example out of the hundred which come to mind will suffice to make this clear.

It is generally easier to make a change of key centre starting from the flat side of the new key and proceeding as in the above case to the sharp side immediately before the establishment of the new key. In this case, looking at the whole passage which is too long to quote, the real modulation is from a G minor key centre to B♭; the introduction of C minor as a vantage-point from which to make the shift of the centre of gravity is a good and very typical example of approach tactics. This use of subsidiary keys in setting up new key centres is of the greatest importance.

Another method of a later period may be mentioned here. The pivot note device, if dwelt upon for a long enough time, can be completely successful as a means of establishing a new key centre. Example 236 is a clear case.

The other matter of technical importance is the use of subsidiary keys and transient modulations as relief from long passages in one key, for example between the re-statement of the first and second subjects in a recapitulation, both of them normally in the tonic. The recapitulation of the first movement of Mozart's piano sonata in D (No. 13) is a good specimen.

The development of what Parry calls 'modulatory digressions' within one key centre, which is in reality only an extension of the use of chromatic harmony, is important at this period, for it is along this road that experiments in modulation continued. Parry's quotation from Mozart is an excellent illustration of his use of the device.

Beethoven carried the use of modulatory digressions further, often using them at the very start of a movement almost before the key centre is established. Most of the works of his middle and last period illustrate this, for example the opening of the E minor piano sonata Op. 90, the beginning of the second *Rasoumoffsky* quartet, or the quartet Op. 95. In all these cases the keys touched remain entirely subordinate to the main key which when it is established comes with added force and definition. This use of initial vagueness of key became a great feature of introductions to movements. Schubert's *Octet* introduction is a good example.

As familiarity with more remote chromatic harmony developed, so, as a natural consequence, did composers experiment more and more with subtler and more distant modulations. Their experiments on the whole followed the basic principles already suggested.

Enough has been said to demonstrate the interdependence of form and key. The main points to sum up are these:

1. The mechanical act of modulation or transition does not in itself establish a new key centre.

2. Within an established key centre modulations and transitions, especially when of short duration or dovetailed, may occur in the same way as chromatic harmony can occur without causing real change of key.

3. These subsidiary modulations may also be used as links in structural modulatory processes where the key centre is changed.

4. It is the real shifts of key centre which are the essential parts of musical structure. Their execution and definition are the factors which control the clarity of form; the balance and timing of their appearance is what gives proportion to it.

Further pursuit of the very important subject of form and modulation is outside the scope of this book. It is a matter for a treatise on composition. What has been said is intended to be merely a pointer for the student; certain basic principles have been suggested; starting from these he may, however much he disagrees with them, investigate for himself the whole problem of key and structure by the close study of actual music. One of the best exercises in key structure is the one which Stanford is said to have set his pupils. It was: 'Using your own thematic material, write a movement on the exact structural scheme of the last movement of Mozart's G minor symphony.' This exercise is strongly recommended to the student; from it he will learn more of key structure and form than from anything else.

Chapter Thirteen

WRITING FOR STRINGS

THE student, who has probably spent most of his time writing for voices, usually finds himself all at sea when asked to write for strings. The first thing he must realize is that in writing for strings he is dealing with a very specialized medium, and he must try to learn something of the characteristics and technique of stringed instruments, and also of the various string ensembles.

A brief sketch of some of the elementary facts about strings is given here. The student should supplement this by studying the appropriate sections of some good books on Orchestration and string technique. (Forsyth's *Orchestration* is as good as any book on the subject.) He must also study the scores of standard string quartets, quintets, etc., and hear the music played.

The workable compass of the various stringed instruments in use to-day, and the open strings are as follows:

Ex. 252.

A few more notes are available in the upward compass of the violin viola and 'cello, both as stopped notes and harmonics. These are better left alone for the present.

This enormous range, compared with the restricted compass of voices, at once opens up new possibilities as well as new responsibilities.

The different tone qualities of the instruments and of their various 'registers' must be fully appreciated by hearing them. To keep the instruments within the normal compass of voices, as students so often do, especially the viola and second violin, is the very negation of string writing.

Clefs. Violin music is written throughout on the ordinary Treble (G) clef. For the viola the Alto (C) clef [alto clef] is normally used. The Treble (G) clef is also employed for passages where leger lines would otherwise become embarrassing. The student should remember that frequent changes of clef are annoying to the player, and only in passages which lie high for a considerable stretch should the Treble clef be emloyed. Three clefs are normally used for the 'cello: the Bass clef [bass clef], the Tenor (C) clef [tenor clef], and the Treble (G) clef. Here again the object is to minimize the number of leger lines. The Bass clef should be used as much as possible; for passages lying entirely above middle C the treble clef (actual sounds) should be employed. Only a few passages lying in the middle of the compass call for the tenor clef [tenor clef with notes]. German writers of the classical period had a tiresome habit of writing high 'cello parts an octave above the actual sounds in the treble clef. This unnecessary complication has now ceased to be fashionable. The double bass uses the normal bass clef and in the higher registers the tenor (C) clef sounding in both cases an octave lower than the actual notes written.

Finger Technique. It has been said that violin technique is a 'technique of position', rather than of notes. This is equally true of the other stringed instruments. Forsyth explains what is meant by a 'technique of position' very clearly, and the student must study this section of his book (*Orchestration*, pp. 305 onwards) with great care if he wants to grasp one of the essential parts of string writing. In doing so he will discover why large leaps which are hazardous and clumsy in keyboard writing, and impossible or ridiculous for voices, are perfectly natural and easy for strings. More will be said on this subject when characteristic string figures are considered; the technical considerations cannot be fully discussed here for reasons of space. Another matter under this heading which the student must study for himself is double, triple, and quadruple stopping. Two notes, if they can be played on adjacent strings, can be sustained; in fact two-part writing for quite extended passages is possible and effective, within the bounds of reasonable technique. Chords may be produced over three or four strings, but with present-day instruments and bows only two of the notes may be sustained. Full lists of triple and quadruple stops will be found in Forsyth. Harmonics both natural (flautato) and artificial should also be explored, as their use adds to the tone colours available as well as to technical possibilities.

Bowing. A great variety of methods of bowing is available on all stringed instruments. Most important, perhaps, is the true bowed legato, an effect which is unrivalled in any other instruments. A perfectly smooth legato, with any kind of attack desired, can be produced and sustained almost indefinitely (as a good player can change the direction of the bow stroke without any noticeable break). Sustained notes of any duration and legato phrases of any length are as easy to strings as they are difficult or impossible to other instruments (except perhaps the organ). The only contingency which makes this real legato impossible is the necessity for a jump over one or two strings by the bow (or a large shift of position) in a phrase like the following:

Ex. 253.

Phrasing of the greatest delicacy and subtlety may be introduced into mainly legato passages, by means of some slight degree of attack at the beginning of a new bow stroke, or some alteration of pressure of the bow or momentary checking of the bow in the middle of a stroke.

Two main types of bowing, with many variations, must be described in some detail. First of all, detached bowing, that is, a change of bow to each note. Ordinary detached bowing in quick and moderately quick passages gives a slightly staccato effect, more pronounced in loud than in soft playing. In slower passages anything from a nearly complete legato to a sharp staccato may be achieved at the will of the player, controlled by the type of attack and release used and the length of the stroke. In detached bowing normally the up (V) and down (⊓) strokes are used alternately. Sometimes for the purpose of achieving the utmost detachment a series of down strokes is used, the bow being lifted off the string after each stroke.

The chief varieties of detached bowing in general use are:

(a) The ordinary detached bowing, with no perceptible check at the end of the stroke, which may be a whole bow length or less according to

the duration of the note and dynamic requirement, each note receiving a slight attack at the turning of the bow. No bowing signs required,

(b) Detached bowing with a definite break at the end of each stroke (the normal bowed staccato). Simply write dots above (or below) each note, without a slur.

(c) The *Sautillé*. A very useful and common form of light staccato bowing, in which only the middle of the bow is used and allowed to rebound quite gently on the strings (alternate down and up bows for each note). Most professional players use this form of bowing for quick, light and quiet detached staccato passages. Its dynamic range is *ppp* to *mp*. No special notation is used beyond the dot.

(d) Extreme staccato, made by a series of consecutive down bows, the bow being lifted from the string at the end of each stroke and replaced at the heel. This form of bowing is specially effective in double and triple stops; it is more frequently found in orchestral work than in chamber music. It is indicated by a series of ⊓ or ⊔ signs.

(e) The *Martelé*. A short bow stroke in which the bow is abruptly stopped on the string, instantly checking the vibration. The point (or less commonly the heel) of the bow is used in alternate down and up strokes. Both *p* and *f* are equally effective. The result is a hard precise staccato. The sign used is ▾ sometimes reinforced with the direction *Martelé*.

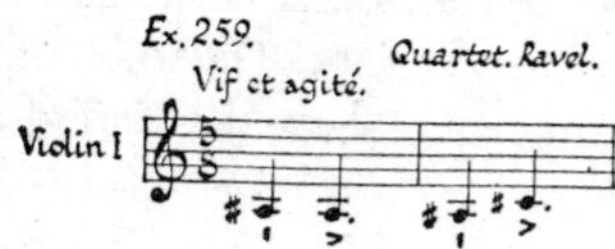

The second type of bowing is that in which groups of notes are played in one bow (up or down).

(a) The true bowed legato, indicated by a slur (which, it may be observed here, has nothing to do with the long phrase marks of vocal or keyboard writing) placed over the notes to be played in each stroke, has already been mentioned. The number of notes which can be played in one stroke depends upon the speed of the notes and their dynamic intensity. Two bars of $\frac{4}{4}$ time 'moderato' *mf–f* is a reasonable maximum, or four bars *pp–p*. Changes of direction of the bow stroke can be made, as has been pointed out, almost unnoticed.

(b) The *Louré*. This is usually an up-bow stroke, in which several notes are played, pressure being exerted on the bow for each note and a very slight check made after each. Forsyth describes it as 'a slightly detached cantabile in which each note receives a definite pressure from the bow'. The number of notes which can be played this way in one stroke is limited to four or five. The notation is: . The *Louré* effect can also be obtained in detached bowing.

(c) Slurred Staccato. A group of notes, often rapid, may be played staccato in one bow stroke by good players. An up bow is almost always used, the bow being checked from the wrist.

A considerable amount of space has been devoted to bowing technique, as it is a most essential part of string writing. The student should get into the habit of bowing his string writing from the very start, and for this purpose he must gain practical experience of the different effects obtainable, either as performer or close observer. Only in this way can he begin to think musically in terms of strings. The study of scores is also essential. A short Beethoven example will show the kind of thing that is meant by good bowing.

Some short passages from Beethoven's *Rasoumoffsky Quartets* are given at the end of this chapter. The student may find it useful to 'bow' these himself, and then examine the bowing in the scores.

Repeated and sustained notes. Repeated notes, which in vocal work are difficult and ineffective unless backed up by changes of syllable, are extremely useful in string writing. Both these and long sustained notes with their expressive and rhythmic possibilities are a basic part of this technique. Repeated notes at any speed from the tremolo downwards, and with any accentuation, rhythm, and dynamic intensity, are easily played. The various types of bowing available should be studied in Forsyth. The following example shows some of the musical possibilities:

The various forms of tremolo are so essentially a part of string figuration that a few more words must be said about them.

(a) The Bowed Tremolo. This implies rapid reiteration of a note with very short bow strokes (down and up). Sforzandos and < > are very effective.

(b) The Fingered Tremolo. The rapid alternation of two notes (not more than an augmented fourth apart) without change of bow.

(c) The Bowed and Fingered Tremolo. Tremolo down and up strokes on notes on the same string or adjacent strings in rapid alternation.

The details of notation and technique may be studied in Forsyth.

Pizzicato: Mutes: and other devices.

Instead of being set in vibration by the bow, the strings may be plucked with the fingers of the right hand. This is an extremely useful and characteristic device in string writing. Especially effective is the pizzicato bass ('cello or C.B.).

Quite quick passages may be played pizzicato with good effect.

Pizzicato chords are very telling if used judiciously.

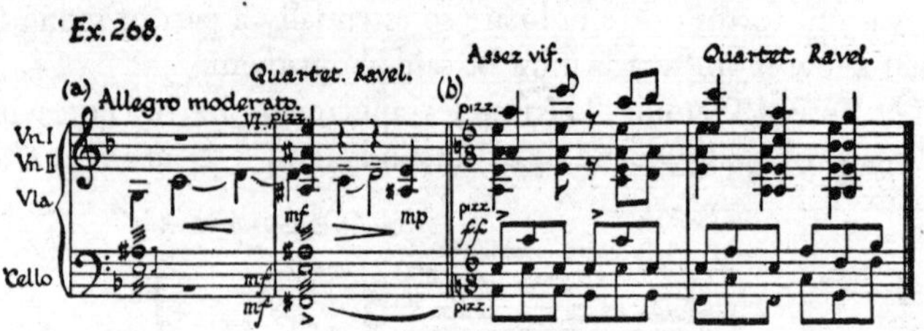

High notes, especially on the violin, are ineffective '*pizz*', as the length of string is not sufficient to produce satisfactory vibrations by this method, and the result is rather a dry snap than a note. It is possible for special effects.

'*Pizz*' is the indication for plucking the strings, and '*arco*' for the return to the bow. The change over can be achieved very rapidly, especially at the end of an up-bow.

Stringed instruments may be 'muted' (indication: *con sord*, French *sourd*) by means of a device touching the bridge which damps the vibrations. A curious and characteristic tone results, which is useful and beautiful in small doses. Considerable time is required in the middle of a piece to fix the mute. Taking it off (*senza sord*) is a quicker process.

Ex. 269.

Andantino. ♪ = 80 Quartet. Slow movt. Debussy.

Vn. I / Vn. II sourd pp; Viola / 'Cello sourd p

Adagio molto e mesto.
4
Vn I
molto cantabile pp
ibid. 3rd Movt.
cresc.
p cresc.
sfp
cresc.
sfp
dim.
ibid. last movt.
5
Allegro. Theme russe.
Cello
sempre p
p
6
ibid.
Vn I
p
dim.
pp
sempre p
7
Molto adagio.
String Quartet Op.59 No.2
Vn I
p
cresc.
f
p
Slow movt. Beethoven
ibid. 3rd movt.
8
Allegretto.
Vn I
pp
cresc
f
9
Allegretto.
ibid.
Vla
p
cresc
sf
10
Allegro vivace
String Quartet Op.59 No.3. 1st movt. Beethoven
f

Chapter Fourteen

WRITING FOR STRINGS (CONTINUED): CHARACTERISTIC STRING FIGURES

VOICES are in the main a melodic medium of musical expression; strings combine rhythmic and harmonic with melodic possibilities. Moreover strings are far more agile than voices both in the ease with which they can play intervals, speed of articulation of notes, and range. Such a phrase as the following, which would be ridiculous for voices, is perfectly natural on a violin:

A careful study of the scores of string chamber music will disclose certain characteristic string figures. These fall under three rough headings: (a) Rhythmic; (b) Broken Chords (harmonic); (c) Melodic. Two or even all three of these factors are usually combined in some measure. The following short examples may help the student to get some idea of the variety of string figuration available.

(a) *Rhythmic Figures*

(b) *Arpeggio ('broken chord') Figures*

Arpeggio (plus Rhythmic)

(c) *Melodic (plus Arpeggio).*

Ex. 282.

Melodic (plus rhythmic)

Ex. 283.

These are, of course, only a few of the types of string figuration. The student should also explore the possibilities of the various forms of tremolo described on page 151, and figures derived from these.

String Ensembles. The essence of good string ensemble writing is that each instrument should play its characteristic and individual part in the whole. Whether it is playing a tune, developing some figure, or merely supplying a rhythmic or arpeggio accompaniment, it must be contributing something essential and characteristic to the music as a whole. It might be argued from this that string writing is necessarily contrapuntal. This is true in so far as any independent part writing is, in a sense, contrapuntal; but individual parts of string ensembles are generally more harmonic than contrapuntal in the stricter sense.

Crossing of parts. Students often have a curious complex about what is referred to in text-books as 'crossing of parts', which they try to avoid as if it were one of the seven deadly sins. Such inhibitions must be exorcized once and for all. Even in the purest vocal writing (Palestrina) complete

Ex. 284.

freedom of each individual part to go where it pleases within its compass is an essential feature of the technique. In fact the full exploration of the different registers of the voices probably accounts for much of the amazing richness and effectiveness of sixteenth-century polyphony. This applies in even greater degree to string ensembles. The individual instruments must be given complete freedom throughout their compass. A well-known instance of the intensity of effect which may be produced by crossing of parts is to be found in the opening bars of the last movement of Tschaikovsky's sixth symphony. (Ex. 284).

The following short extracts from examples of different kinds of string writing are worth looking at in some detail as a preliminary to a close study of every string quartet and quintet score which the student can find.

(I.)

These two fragments from the scherzo of Haydn's Quartet in D, Op. 33, No. 6, show string quartet writing at its simplest, and in some ways most charming. Notice the rests, which lighten the texture and add point to the imitative entries in the first fragment, and the sudden four-part harmony in the second. The musical content of the first example is just a five-note rhythmic and melodic figure treated imitatively in all the parts. This example shows another important point. Imitation to be effective need not be exact; in fact it is usually very much more effective when it is not. Here all the entries may be said to be imitative, yet not one is an exact imitation. The second extract is just a 'cello figure with the simplest and lightest possible rhythmic accompaniment. Yet the result is in its way perfect string quartet writing. The figures are all typical string figures. The lay-out of the parts deserves careful study. Notice the wide gap between the 'cello and the part above it (second violin); the close position of the two violin parts; and the spacing of the harmonies in the last three bars.

In this Mozart example the texture is almost as simple as in the Haydn. The emotional content of the music is very much more intense There is a much more complex harmonic structure, and more contrast and independence in the rhythms of the different instruments. Rhythmic imitation is still in the foreground, but it has greater variety and the parts have a more definite melodic curve.

The harmonic structure should be analysed, and the harmonic rhythm noticed. The judicious use of rests and the long sustained notes in the 'cello part is important.

The whole quartet will repay the closest study. It contains some of the most beautiful and moving music Mozart ever wrote, and is string quartet writing at its very best.

(3)

This quotation from the slow movement of Beethoven's second *Rasoumoffsky Quartet* shows a much more complex texture. Special notice should be taken of the bowing: long slow bows in *piano* passages; staccato notes with rests in between in one bow; the contrast of the detached ♩. ♬ ♩ figure in the viola. All this is characteristic string writing.

The lay-out is important; for example, the wide gap between the viola and the second violin in bars 2 and 3, which in writing for voices would sound thin, and the crossing of parts.

There is very great melodic and rhythmic independence of individual instruments and groups of instruments.

(4)

Ex. 289.

Adagio. Op. 163. Schubert.

pp espressivo

pp

pp

pp

1st 'cello

2nd 'cello

pizz. pp

This beautiful opening of the slow movement of Schubert's string quintet is a good example of string 'lay-out'. The second violin, viola, and first 'cello take care of the melodic line and its harmony, over a pizzicato bass, while the first violin has a decorative figure. The movement abounds in the most exquisitely wrought decoration, especially in the last four pages, a passage too long to quote here.

(5)

This example, from Brahms's late string quintet shows the antiphonal use of violins and violas over a typical arpeggio figure in the 'cello. Notice the use of rests and dovetailing of the melodic phrases.

These few bars from Wolf's *Italian Serenade* are a striking example of freedom in lay-out and independence in quartet writing. The student should notice carefully (though perhaps he had better not emulate in examinations) the 'doubling' between the two violins.

(7)

This opening of Ravel's string quartet, shows the medium used very expressively. It is a good example of the range and sweep of melodic writing characteristics of string ensembles.

From these few examples in different styles, some 'hints' may be underlined:

1. Rests let daylight into the texture. They also give point to entries and imitations. Do not keep all the instruments going all the time.

2. Careful spacing of parts and general lay-out are essential to good string writing. Do not keep the parts close together all the time. Wide gaps are often good, and need not be confined to the lowest two parts.

3. The pizzicato bass is a useful and beautiful device.

4. Imitations need not be exact.

Chapter Fifteen

WRITING FOR STRINGS (CONTINUED): HARMONIZATION OF SHORT MELODIES FOR STRING COMBINATIONS

1. IF the student has read the previous chapter carefully, and studied the scores of some representative string works and listened to these works adequately played, he may have acquired some idea of what is meant by string writing. He must now apply this idea to short exercises. To do this he must first be able to harmonize any normal melody naturally and convincingly. The first thing to do in any exercise where an upper part is given, is to add a simple bass.

In the above example, a simple binary melody (Vn I) is taken and a sketch bass is added which indicates fairly clearly the obvious modulations, and also gives a good idea of the harmonic rhythm. This last point is important. Nearly all students over-harmonize their melodies (that is, change the harmony too often). Another common fault is a sudden change of the harmonic rhythm for no good purpose. The best way to find the normal harmonic rhythm of a melody is by this process of adding a simple bass with the fewest changes of harmony possible. (It is assumed that the student has got to the stage when he can recognize passing notes, accented and unaccented, and other unessential notes, with certainty.) The normal basic rate of harmonic change in the example we are discussing is 'one harmony to a bar'. At the approach to cadences (for example, bars 7, and 13–17) and in modulations, a quicker rate of harmonic change may be necessary or desirable, and a certain amount of variety is good. The kind of thing that is really bad is a sudden variation in the speed of harmonic change and harmonization of obvious unessential notes like the following:

Spacing of harmony is a first essential of musicianship second only to the necessity for being able to choose the right chord and progression The next step is to produce some kind of characteristic string texture.

In the completed version of this exercise a simple string texture on the harmonic basis given (with a slight variation in bar 3) has been aimed at. Obviously a much more contrapuntal texture could easily have been found. (For example the melody will go in canon for about four bars beginning on F on the third beat of bar 1.) A simple melody like this does not seem to call for such complications, so a straightforward treatment has been kept. Some imitation has been used in bars 9–12, not for its own sake, but because it seems to fit in naturally and add a certain amount of interest.

2. The previous working is an attempt to show a very simple type of writing which is to some extent characteristic of strings. A rather more elaborate type may now be attempted, making use of 'figures' taken from the given 'part'.

The first step, as before, must be to make sure of the natural harmony and modulation of the melody, by adding a rudimentary bass. The next step is to examine the given part for possible 'figures' and imitations.

The minim seems to be the natural harmonic unit, as the time signature suggests, and though many bars will not require two harmonies to the bar, more than two harmonies will be rare (i.e. changes of harmony on crotchet beats). Three possible 'figures' for use are immediately apparent: (a) is a useful '*lead*'; (b) has melodic possibilities; (c) looks as if it might be useful for purposes of accompaniment.

A sketch on the following lines may now be made:

The harmony in bar 2 has been altered; a 'G' bass gives more point to the 'F' in the given part which now becomes a seventh (either essential or appoggiatura). It also makes the figure (c) more natural and complete. A $^6_3$ on F would be very tame after the initial figure (c). In bar 13 another slight change of harmony to a G minor chord makes the inversion of figure (c) available.

The third stage is to fill in the parts making use of the harmonic basis and points of imitation as far as these will go naturally and easily.

3. The working of an independent accompanimental figure is such an important part of string writing that the student should give it careful consideration. It is obvious that only a fairly small percentage of melodies is suitable for this kind of treatment. It is also rather difficult to manage and calls for a certain degree of contrapuntal skill and facility.

A melody for which this type of working might be suitable is given below. A possible accompanimental figure is hinted at in bar 8.

Bars 9–13 present a difficulty which calls for musicianship and some imagination. The piece as a whole may be regarded as four four-bar phrases. The second phrase in the given part overruns by half a bar, and then after a bar's rest there is a fragmentary entry before the recapitulation of the opening. Some other part must take up the 'melody' at bar 9 with a new phrase overlapping the first violin phrase. Another difficulty in places like this is key control. The key scheme must be worked out carefully. Bar 8 is obviously in C (relative major). Bar 9 indicates modulation to D minor in bar 10. Bars 11–12 touch F major. Bar 13 returns to A minor.

Some such working as the following might be acceptable:

Ex. 300.
Andante moderato.
Vn. I
Vn. II
Vla I
Vla II
'Cello
mf espress.
p
p
mf espress.
pizz p
arco
mf
f

rall.
rall.
rall.
rall.
pizz.
rall.
arco

Melodies for harmonization in the way suggested in section 1.

Melodies for harmonization in the style suggested in §2.
Vn I. Allegro.
1
p
cresc.
mf
cresc.
f
dim.
p
Moderato.
2
mf
p
cresc.
f
p
Con moto.
3
f
dim.
mp cresc.
f
Rather slowly.
4
p
mf
f
cresc.
ff
dim.
f
mf
p
pp
Moderato.
5
f

Lento.
6
p
cresc.
f

7 Complete the following as a String Quartet. (§2)
Andante con moto.
f
sf
mf
Vn I
p
pp
mp

Melodies for harmonization in the style suggested in § 3. (use of an accompanying figure)
1 for 2 violins, viola and 2 'celli.
Quintet in C. Slow Movt. Schubert.
2nd Vn
pp espressivo
cresc.
f
p
pp
cresc.
f
decresc.
p
pp
dim
ppp
f
dim. p
pp
ppp
dim.
2 String Quartet.
Extract from slow movt. of Quartet Op. 59 No. 2.
Beethoven.
Molto adagio.
sempre stacc.
Vn I
p
Vn II
ten.
cresc.
f
p
cresc.
Full close in B maj.
3 String Quintet.
Rather slow.
Vn I
p
cresc.
f
pp
p
mf
f
pp

4 For String Quintet.

5 Strings, 4, 5, or 6 parts.

6 String Quintet.

Further exercises in writing for string ensembles will be found among the 'papers' at the end of the book.

Chapter Sixteen

PIANOFORTE ACCOMPANIMENT

STUDENTS generally find considerable difficulty in writing pianoforte accompaniments to given melodies. To be able to do this really well ought to be part of every good musician's equipment, yet it seems to have been a sadly neglected study in the past.

The fact that the majority of students are pianists in some degree does not seem to give them any pianistic sense when it comes to writing down notes. It should, however, help them to see what can and cannot be done at the keyboard with one pair of hands.

It is not proposed to give a detailed account of the technical side of pianoforte writing here. Material for study from Haydn and Mozart to Ravel is readily available, and the student may, by careful observation, learn what pianoforte writing really is.

For the present purpose (i.e. accompaniment) a few general observations on pianoforte style will suffice.

1. Pianoforte writing must not be thought of as being for a definite number of 'voices'. Except in music of the contrapuntal period and its survivals (fugues and definitely contrapuntal movements) the tendency of keyboard writing has been towards a harmonic texture. Pianoforte writing will be vertical rather than horizontal in its outlook; the progressions will be from chord to chord rather than from note to note in a 'part'.

2. The pianoforte, it must be remembered, is largely a percussive instrument. It cannot sustain long notes as can strings or wind instruments or, within limits, voices; nor can it 'sing' a sustained melodic line in the same way (although judicious pedalling and legato playing can make up much of the deficiency in this respect). Rhythmic figuration will therefore enter largely into good pianoforte texture. The development of 'figures', rhythmic, harmonic, and melodic, will form a large part of pianoforte accompaniment.

3. Lay-out and spacing of the actual notes is most vitally important. The pianoforte has an enormous range, and the student must acquaint himself with the possibilities of this by practical experiment. He must also try out for himself chords in various positions and in different registers.

In writing an accompaniment to a given melody the first thing to do is to harmonize the melody simply and naturally (as in the case of string quartets and all work of this kind). The fewer changes of harmony in a bar the better. To grasp the essential harmonic rhythm of the melody is the first necessity. This has been said before in this book, but it can hardly be said too often.

The accompaniment should generally be self-sufficient; that is, it should make harmonic sense by itself as well as with the melody. The bass of the accompaniment, therefore, will almost always be the real bass of the whole work. On rare occasions the solo part may also be the real bass (by doubling the accompaniment bass), and on even rarer ones may stand as a bass by itself, over which an independent accompaniment, sometimes a single strand of melody, may be written; but in nine cases out of ten the bass of the accompaniment will be a real bass of both the melody and pianoforte part. The superstructure of the accompaniment will be free within the normal limits of technique and may reinforce the melody as desired.

The weight and complexity of the pianoforte part will be dictated largely by the character of the melody. A vigorous melody (for example, some string solo parts) will generally call for an economical accompaniment; a quieter one may require more movement in the pianoforte part. The choice of exactly the right form of accompaniment for a given melody, either vocal or instrumental, requires real imagination and musicianship as well as inventive capacity and technical ability. It is therefore a most valuable part of any student's training.

More will be said in the next chapter about getting the atmosphere of words in the accompaniment. Serious song has long ceased to be a tune with an accompaniment of the Alberti bass type. The accompaniment has become an integral part of the song.

The first difficulty which faces the beginner is the selection and working of 'figures'. The following simple examples of pianoforte accompaniment at its best may give the student some idea of what to aim at.

I.

Ex. 301 Cradle Song. Schubert.

Slow

Voice

Piano

This short passage is taken from one of the simplest and most beautiful of Schubert's songs. The swaying accompaniment figure is perfectly pianistic, and perfectly fitting the subject and melody. The important things to notice are: (1) the extreme simplicity of the harmony; (2) the lay-out and spacing of the pianoforte part; (3) the way in which the accompanimental figure is worked. It does not go on relentlessly the whole time, but is relieved by plain harmony (for example in bar 5). (4) The effective 'shadow-doubling' of the voice part in bar 4; (5) The little coda developed from the rhythm of the solo part in bar 2.

In this splendid song Brahms uses a characteristic syncopated accompanimental figure. The whole song should be studied with the greatest care, for, as well as being one of the best songs Brahms wrote, the accompaniment is a model of pianoforte writing of its kind. In bar 5 the delayed shadowing of the melody should be noticed; this is a very telling device. In bar 6 the change to quaver rest/quaver is a good touch.

The variety of possible figuration and working of figures is of course endless. Some examples of various types will be given later in this chapter. In working figures a mistake which is often made is to start one figure, work it for a few bars, then drop it completely and start another repeating the process *ad lib.* It is equally dangerous to work one single figure without relief (unless it is a very good one). It is often a good thing to drop a figure altogether for a bar or two, as in the Schubert song quoted above. By studying Schubert's method of relieving a figure in such songs as *Gretchen am Spinnrade, Erl King, To be Sung on the Water*, the best solution to the problem may be found.

SOME TECHNICAL CONSIDERATIONS

1. It has been pointed out that the bass of the accompaniment is generally the real bass of the whole work. What are its responsibilities in relation to (a) the solo part, and (b) the rest of the accompaniment with regard to such things as consecutives, hidden and actual? The general tendency in the great song writers seems to be to regard the whole accompaniment as a complete entity, with the solo part as a separate 'obbligato', both being mutually interdependent. The analogy of 'double choir' writing in which ideally each choir is complete in itself yet co-ordinated with the other, may help if not pushed too far.

It will generally be found that the bass behaves itself with due propriety (within the limits of good pianoforte technique) in relation to the top 'part' of the accompaniment at least. In its relation to the solo part much less puritanical behaviour is often observed; for example, bar 1 of Schubert's *Cradle Song* quoted above. Notice that the accompaniment by itself is unexceptionable technically, but the behaviour of the bass and melody is rather less discreet. The student will not cramp his style seriously if he denies himself these liberties, at any rate till he knows what he is doing, and regards the solo part as another outside part (if it differs from the top part of the accompaniment).

Short patches of doubling the solo part in the accompaniment bass are almost always crude. Whole phrases doubled in this way are better. Hidden consecutives between solo and bass, unless well covered up by the accompaniment, are usually amateurish.

2. The accompaniment bass, if it is the real bass of the whole work, is responsible for the harmonic progression just as in four-part vocal writing. Here is to be found one of the big traps in pianoforte writing.

It may be stated as a general principle that rests do not cancel a harmony until the next harmonic accent (that is normally the next strong beat or secondary accent). The following passage is obviously completely wrong:

The pitch of the bass in pianoforte writing is important in this connexion. It must be realized that the effect of one bass note lasts either till the next normal harmonic accent or until it is replaced by another bass note in the same register. The following version, whether written with a rest as in bar 1 or without as in bar 2, is almost as bad as that quoted above:

The same principle applies to upper 'parts'. If the melody has a rest on a beat of the bar which does not naturally carry a relatively strong harmonic accent in the context (i.e. where a change of harmony is not expected) and the accompaniment changes harmony on that beat, the result, unless the melody note preceding the rest is part of the new harmony, will be crude and unsatisfactory.

3. The relation of the solo part (provided it is not the real bass or coincident with it) to the superstructure of the accompaniment is quite free. It must be remembered that the solo part is of a different timbre from the accompaniment and so achieves a considerable measure of emancipation. It can therefore be doubled, ornamented, and shadowed quite freely in the pianoforte part without losing its identity. (See Examples 301, bars 5 and 6; 302, bars 5–7.)

Nevertheless, in certain circumstances care is necessary, particularly when dealing with suspensions, appoggiaturas, and discords. When complete doubling happens for considerable stretches (especially at the unison) little trouble is likely to occur, but momentary doubling of dissonances, and the sounding of the note of resolution against a suspension or appoggiatura need care and discretion if they are not to sound crude or at least muddy. The contrast between the solo and the piano does, however, mitigate things, and goes some way towards clarifying the muddles which this kind of shady technique generally implies, and which would be intolerable in four-part vocal writing.

4. A word may be said about the superstructure of the pianoforte part itself. Since pianoforte writing does not normally imply real part writing, consecutives (even sporadic) within the superstructure cease to be objectionable. The superstructure had best be treated as an entity which must make good harmonic sense with the bass, and the solo part.

The following short fragments may serve to give the student an idea of the types of figuration which are frequently found in pianoforte accompaniment. They should be studied carefully as a preliminary to an intensive diet of the best serious songs from Schubert to Vaughan Williams, and the repertoire of violin and piano, and 'cello and piano music.

b.
Andante con espress.
'True Love!'
Op.7 No.1. Brahms.
Voice
p
Piano
pp
con ped.
c.
Vivace.
'The Vain Suit.'
Op. 84 No.4. Brahms.
Voice
Piano
p legg.

d
Quickly
The Maid of the Mill. 1.
Op.25. Schubert.
Voice
Piano
p
mf

Allegro moderato.
Violin Sonata in G. 1st Movt
Op. 96. Beethoven.
e
rit.
a tempo
Violin
Piano

Ex. 307.

2. Simple chord figures. (Rhythmic)

Vivace ma non troppo.
Violin Sonata in G. Op.78. Brahms.
e.
Violin
pp grazioso
dol.
Piano
pp grazioso
Ex.308.
3. Melodic and rhythmic figures
'The Monkeys Carol'. Op.175. Stanford.
Allegretto.
Voice
Kind Christian souls who pass me by On bus--i-ness in tent.
Piano
p
'We wandered.' Op.94. No2. Brahms.
Andante espressivo.
Voice
Piano

'To be sung on the water.' Schubert.

Allegro moderato.
Voice
pp
Piano
pp

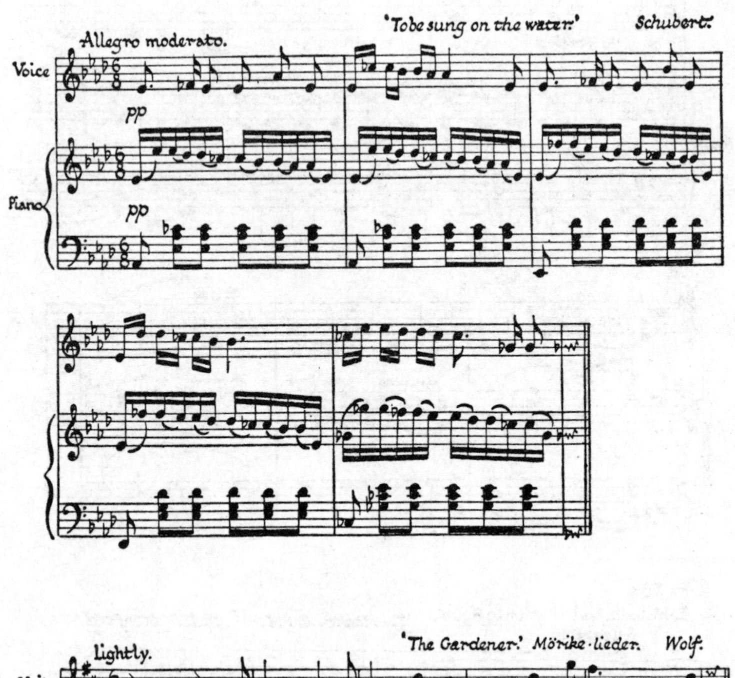

'The Gardener.' Mörike-lieder. Wolf.

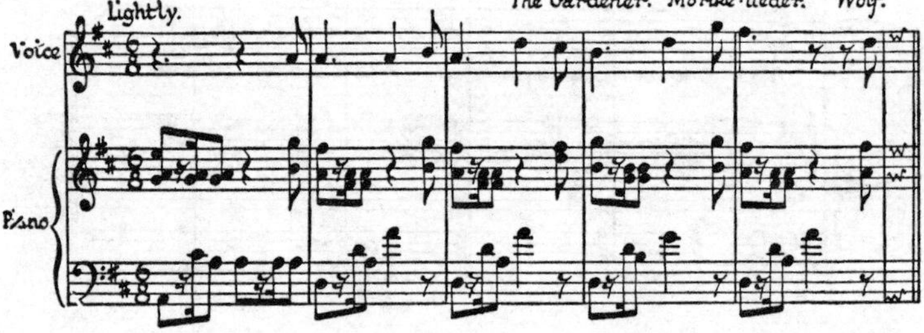
Lightly.
Voice
Piano

Exercises.
Complete the following.
Die Schöne Mullerin. Schubert.
1
Rather slow.
Voice
p
pp
3
2
Andante.
'The Sandman' Brahms.
Voice
pp
pp
3
Lento ma non troppo.
'Parting' Op. 19. Brahms.

Add piano accompaniments to the following:

Some further exercises will be found in the 'papers' at the end of the book.

Chapter Seventeen

SETTING WORDS TO MUSIC

THIS book does not pretend to be a treatise on composition. It often happens, however, that students have a very creditable wish to try out the technique they have acquired in writing songs; indeed the somewhat peremptory order to the Muse: 'Set the following words for solo voice with piano accompaniment,' or 'as a part song for four voices' is unhappily too frequent in examination papers for the peace of mind of many candidates. It may therefore be of some use to give a few hints on 'setting words to music' here.

ACCENTUATION OF WORDS

The first difficulty which presents itself is the actual underlaying of the words. The 'tyranny of the bar line' with its regular strong and secondary accents in each bar is the chief cause of the trouble.

In the early ages of music, when a single vocal line was the sum total of composition, such rhythm and accentuation as existed was almost entirely verbal. As the art developed, and rudimentary polyphony and 'mensurable music', made definite by the Franconian system of notation, appeared, verbal rhythm still remained the mainspring of music. It was not until polyphony became fairly advanced (in the fifteenth and sixteenth centuries) that harmonic rhythm began to be felt in any definite form.

In considering sixteenth-century polyphony it is probably safe to say that there is a definite measured harmonic rhythm against which the melodic strands move with almost complete rhythmic freedom. This implies unfettered verbal rhythm and accentuation against a stable harmonic rhythmic basis; it provides ample scope for real speech rhythm and cross rhythms which composers of to-day strive, usually in vain, to recapture by frequent changes of time signature, and various other devices.

With the development of the harmonic and instrumental aspect of music in the seventeenth century, harmonic rhythm became increasingly dominant and the tyranny of the bar line more and more firmly established. The way in which English composers of the Restoration period dealt with the problem at a comparatively early stage in its real existence will be touched upon later.

The eighteenth century saw an even greater rigidity in rhythmic formality. Following the lead of Handel in England, composers began to treat words as little more than pegs on which to hang their music; the general impression is often that the words have been fitted on to the music in a haphazard way with little or no regard for declamation or accentuation. The 'tyranny of the bar line' reigned supreme at the expense of verbal accentuation except in recitative passages, and its influence persists to this day.

Through the nineteenth century the maltreatment of words went from bad to worse. The revival of interest in Tudor music and folk song in the present century seems to have made composers once more conscious of the rhythm and accentuation of the English language as their efforts to give proper declamation to words, and escape from the bar line tyranny show.

The problem of setting English words to measured music is really one of adapting free and irregular verbal rhythms to measured and regular musical rhythms. Actually the difficulty is by no means insurmountable, as the Restoration composers and some of their successors were able to show. It must be remembered in considering their achievements in this direction that a good deal of 'Tudor' technique remained as a recent part of their inheritance, and as a result of this the maximum regularity of time signature rhythm was not yet in fashion. In a fairly regular barred rhythm they did in fact manage to achieve almost perfect verbal declamation, as the following examples will show:

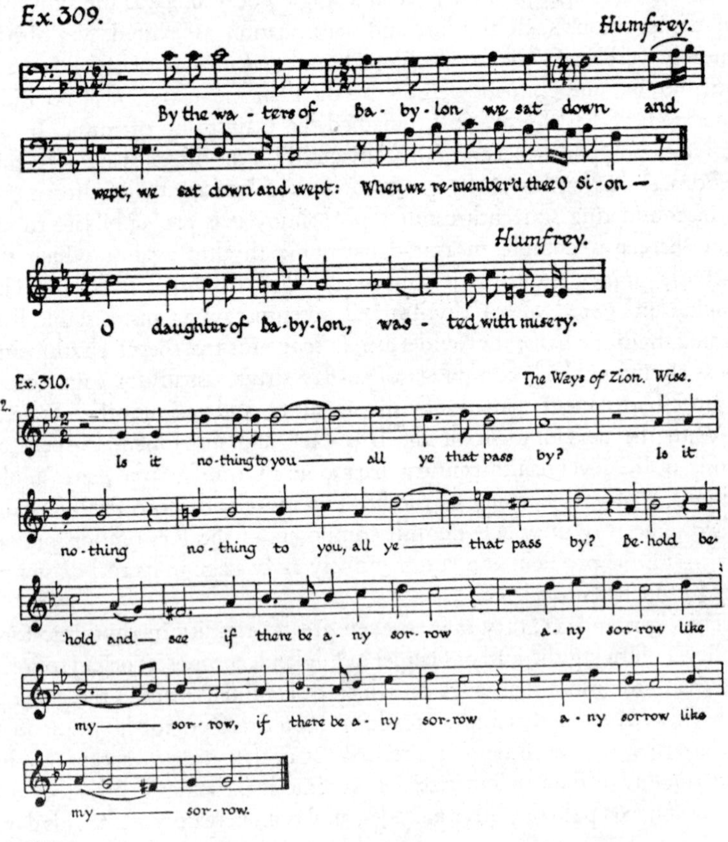

If the student examines these quotations carefully, he may learn the three most important rhythmic factors of setting words: (1) good verbal accentuation; (2) giving the right weight and duration to each syllable; (3) the proper placing of each word in the rise and fall of the melodic line. These three factors are very much bound up together, but it may help to say a few words about each aspect by itself.

1. By verbal accentuation is meant the actual accent which each syllable receives. In tackling this problem the first thing to do is to make quite sure of the rhythm of the words to be set. Poetry will have an underlying quantitative metre, with a superimposed rhythm of accent. Prose rhythm will be solely a matter of stress. Good declamation will help the student to grasp the rhythm of words and he must make up his mind exactly how every line or sentence should be declaimed before starting to set words to music.

It is by no means difficult to find musical notation which will reproduce verbal rhythm exactly (Recit); the problem is to wed verbal rhythm and metre to their musical counterparts so that each remains convincing.

Take first of all a simple metrical example (accent rhythm shown on top: quantity rhythm below this):

The silver Swan who living had no note,

When death approached unlocked her silent throat;

Leaning her breast against the reedy shore

Thus sung her first and last, and sung no more:

'Farewell all joys, O death come close mine eyes,

More Geese than Swans now live, more fools than wise.'

The metrical scheme of the first two lines is perfectly obvious. It might be expressed musically thus:

The verbal rhythm and accentuation might be transcribed as follows:

It is obvious that neither of these will do for a musical setting. Gibbons's solution to the problem is about as perfect as it can be.

2. It becomes obvious that the length of a note has almost as much influence on its accentuation as its position in the bar. The really important accents in the above setting fall mostly on relatively long notes (for example in the third line the word breast on a dotted minim makes the accent on '-gainst', even though it is a first beat of a bar, relatively weak). The exception is the word 'death': this being the first accented note in a new phrase receives a naturally full accent. (There is a definite tendency to expect a relatively strong accent early in a new phrase.) Another interesting point in this connexion is the effect of the dotted crotchets in bars 8 and 15. They both seem to call for a stronger accent than their actual position on the weak second beat of the bar warrants. Pitch here con-

tributes to the accentuation, and there is also the fact that after a rest (i.e. at the beginning of a new phrase) the first relatively strong beat can carry a slightly stronger accent than usual, and here the first note of the phrase is really tied over on to the relatively strong third beat. In both these cases three factors, length of note, position in the phrase, and relative pitch, enable this weak second beat to carry a strong accent.

A long note on a weak beat, however, if it is immediately preceded by a short note on a strong beat need not necessarily carry any accent at all.

Ex. 313.

why seek ye the li - ving a - mong the dead?

The amount of accent taken by a relatively long note is therefore dependent upon its position in the bar and the phrase. Thus can the demands of quantity as well as accent be met.

Ex. 314.

By the wa - ters of Ba - by-lon— we sat down

Ex. 315.

Nei-ther shall sil-ver be weighed for the price thereof

3. The third factor in accentuation is the relative pitch of the note upon which a syllable is placed. An upward leap of a fourth or more gives a natural accent to the higher note. Good singers can, up to a point, lessen this accent, but (except for special effect) it is undesirable to write such a passage as the following:

Ex. 316.

A high note in the compass of a voice at the beginning of a phrase, even on a weak beat, carries a considerable natural accent. The tension required to produce high notes is alone enough to cause this effect, though here again singers can modify the attack in most cases. In the Gibbons setting of the *Silver Swan*, the first note of the phrase 'thus sung her first and last' is very difficult to sing well. Yet it is not so much a miscalculation on Gibbons's part as it looks at first, for the initial stress here and in the last line is much heavier than in the first three lines. In fact the word 'thus' can carry a fairly strong accent, and even more so the word 'more'.

This passage illustrates another very important point. Disjunct movement, anywhere in a phrase, especially leaps as big as fourths and fifths, give considerable extra weight to the notes. A skip downwards to a note brings it into prominence and gives it added accent, though not as much as an upward leap.

The important issue of the relative pitch of notes in the melodic line will be considered from another aspect later. To sum up this section; the three chief factors in accentuation are (1) the position of the note in the bar (whether it falls on a strong, weak, or secondary accent); (2) the relative length of the note; (3) the relative and actual pitch of the note. To these may be added the note's position in the phrase.

One more modern facet of accentuation must be considered. The artificial accent, >. When placed over a note which already bears an accent or potential accent, it merely serves to strengthen that accent. When placed over a note which has no natural claim to an accent it is equivalent to a change of rhythm, and if the accompanying parts do not also change rhythm, a conflict, known as cross rhythm, is set up. This device in music of the harmonic age is an edged tool, and the student should not try to use it till he is very sure of what he is doing. The conflict between the harmonic rhythm and the new verbal rhythm is difficult to manage convincingly, and the result often sounds like a vain attempt to cover up sheer bad accentuation.

THE VOCAL LINE

Stanford has pointed out that the old clefs are an admirable guide to normal range of the voices. He suggests that 'the nearer the average of notes keeps to the middle line of the five, and the closer the vocal part revolves round that as a centre, the better is the tessitura of the song. Leger lines above and below represent the extremes of compass which are to be used more exceptionally and for special effects.'

Ex. 317.

It may, perhaps, be suggested that the present-day tendency is to raise these ranges a little, possibly a tone or semitone.

The rules about forbidden leaps which seem to have found general acceptance in the great age of polyphony (the sixteenth century) are no pedantic prohibitions, but sound common sense. A major sixth, for instance, is very difficult to sing in tune, and so, ungrateful to the singer. Even if sung in tune, it sounds awkward. The student no doubt knows all about the rules of melodic progression. If not he should study them in some good book on sixteenth-century counterpoint.[1] Except for special effect these rules should be followed pretty closely.

A good vocal line is one which is grateful to sing. A voice is not well adapted to leaping about all over the place, and even if a singer can accomplish these gymnastic feats with some equanimity, the result is apt to sound strained and unnatural.

Stanford wrote: 'The poet cannot indicate the pitch or the lilt of his poem, except by the suggestion of the words themselves, and he is obliged to leave all such details, no matter how vital they are to the true rendering of his verse, to the intelligence of the man who reads it. The composer who sets it has, therefore, the great responsibility upon him of interpreting it on the lines which the poet felt, and was unable to write down with the accuracy which is at the musician's command.'

This seems to get to the root of the whole matter. The music the singer sings must not only reproduce the rhythm, accentuation and lilt of the words faithfully; it must mirror the rise and fall, pitch and cadence inherent in them.

Look at the two Boyce examples quoted above. The searching question in the words 'O where shall wisdom be found' is perfectly reproduced by the high note (plus leap) accent on the word 'where' and the rising end of the phrase.

In the fragment 'Neither shall silver be weighed for the price thereof' the lilt of the words 'weighed for the price' is perfectly caught. The rise to the word 'silver' and the weight thrown on the following words by the dotted rhythm, and the finality of the descending end of the sentence all help to bring out the full meaning of the words. At the same time both sentences are good music in themselves.

A word of warning must be given here. Students sometimes become over-conscious of the necessity for mirroring the words in the vocal line, and indulge in extravagant and forced word painting. The word painting, once it makes itself consciously felt by the listener, has gone too far. It

[1] R. O. Morris, *Contrapuntal Technique of Sixteenth Century*, gives a brief but excellent account.

must remain unobtrusively in the background, and be natural and inevitable.

Archbishop Cranmer's campaign for economy in the number of notes placed over a syllable was a sound one. It is specially important in solo song. The days of operatic coloratura are past. Runs, trills, and other vocal gymnastics bring a cheap spectacular element in at once; furthermore they obscure the words, and hold up the action. It must be granted that Bach, Handel, and Purcell (and some others) did remarkable things with florid passages, but the present-day tendency is to get on with the job, and it is a good one. This does not mean that 'one note only to each syllable' is to be the aim and object of the song writer. Two, three, or four notes are often indispensable to the melodic line, and even short melismata can sometimes be wonderfully expressive. The student will of course have to be careful what words he chooses for this form of embellishment. Short and unaccented syllables are impossible, and the vowel sound has to be chosen with some care.

Two types of 'setting words to music' must be considered in some detail: (1) the solo song; (2) unaccompanied choral writing and part song (Chapter 18).

THE SOLO SONG

In the solo song the musical setting (solo voice and accompaniment) must be regarded as a single musical entity, whose function is the artistic interpretation of the words. The accompaniment (if it is there at all) must be an integral part of the whole, and not an *ad lib* extra. It may be a reticent background to the voice part (as, to cite an extreme case, in 'quasi recit.' passages) or of equal importance to it (as in songs such as Schubert's *Erl King*). The ideal is that the three component parts of a song, words, vocal line, and accompaniment (whether it be for piano, string quartet, full orchestra, or any combination) should form a 'team' each contributing its relevant share.

The verse type of song is the simplest form with which we have to deal. This verse-by-verse method of setting words is typical of the folk song and is in some ways the most spontaneous type. Its drawbacks are obvious. The same (or nearly the same) vocal line has to do duty for all the verses of the poem. The rhythmic variations in different verses (and there are bound to be a good many) will have to be met by minor rhythmical changes in the melody, and the possibilities of such changes are often not great enough to cope with much rhythmic freedom in the words. This at once limits the choice of words for this kind of setting to poems in which the verses are all metrically consistent, with relatively little rhythmic variation. The second drawback is that changes of mood in the verse-by-verse setting can only be reflected in the accompaniment, or by alteration of speed in the musical setting. (For the moment we will rule out change of mode or key.) This imposes further limitation on choice of words, as it implies emotional consistency in all the verses and no great range or sudden change of mood.

It would seem then that the verse-by-verse type of song is best adapted for poetry of a simple and direct character, of the ballad or folk-song type. Yet it must be remembered that within the limits of this kind of song many masterpieces of a complex and highly organized kind exist such as Schubert's *Auf dem Wasser zu singen* (Op. 72), Brahms's *Sapphic Ode*, as well as the many beautiful folk songs and simply constructed songs such as Schubert's *Cradle Song* and, to mention one out of many fine modern English examples, Butterworth's *Is my team ploughing?*

In writing this type of song great care must be taken with the voice part, and it must be borne in mind that with only minor alterations it has to do duty for all the verses. This rules out vivid declamation and 'point making'. Another important thing is that the melody must be able to stand on its own merits, and bear repetition; if its harmonic implication is too colourful it will soon pall and lose its point. It is obvious that in shaping such a melody all the verses to be set must be carefully considered. The general mood and feeling of the poem as a whole, rather than the content of any single line or verse, must be the dominating factor. The melody itself must have shapeliness and it must be musically satisfying. A study of our own folk song at its best will show the student how to write this kind of melody.

A variation of the verse song which has proved itself to be of great value, is a kind of compromise between the strict verse-by-verse setting and the 'durch-componiert' or continuous setting (which will be considered in the next section). This may range from comparatively simple alteration in the rhythm, actual notes, or mode or key of the melody in different verses, to the wholesale interpolation of new material for some of the verses. The procedure in such cases will be dictated by the words.

The most valuable preparatory exercise for writing verse songs is the arrangement of folk songs. It is also excellent practice in writing piano-accompaniment.

Most of our folk songs have a strong modal background, especially noticeable at the cadences. It is not suggested that modal harmony (whatever that strangely anomalous expression may mean) should be exclusively employed in setting folk songs. But the modal atmosphere of the melody should be given due consideration and jarring anachronisms avoided just as much as self-conscious archaisms.

The Continuous ('Durch-componiert') Song. (The 'Art Song' of Parry's *Art of Music.*)

In this type of song the function of the music is the complete interpretation of the words; the setting must bring out the full meaning of the words and their atmosphere, and at the same time create a musical work of art.

The form of such songs will be dictated largely by the words. It will vary from such complex structures as Schubert's *Erl King* to songs of such outward simplicity but intensity of feeling as his *Death and the Maiden.*

Perhaps the best example for preliminary study is Schubert's superb *Gretchen am Spinnrade.* This marvellous song fulfils all the ideals of 'the art song'. It is not only a wonderful setting of the words; it is great music. The accompaniment pictures the scene perfectly. The vocal line follows the emotional variation of the words most graphically. The sense of climax and shape is completely satisfying; the first (emotional) climax taking the form of a dramatic stopping of the spinning-wheel motif in the accompaniment, followed by a recapitulation with an even more forceful dramatic climax and a quiet coda.

It is impossible to teach anyone how to write songs of this type (or of any other kind for that matter), but a few hints and warnings may be of use.

1. The setting must be the direct outcome of the composer's feeling for the words. It must be his interpretation of them. Its value will depend upon the quality of his feeling and his power to translate that experience into music.

2. The voice part and accompaniment are the vehicles for giving musical expression to the words. If it is remembered that the voice part should grow naturally out of the words, and that the words are not just a peg on which to hang the melody, it is unlikely that its independent purely musical interest will get out of proportion. The accompaniment is more in danger of doing this. There is a risk of songs in some cases becoming piano (or orchestral) tone poems, with a sort of vocal recitative going on in the background as a commentary or explanation. The result may be good music, but it is certainly not good song.

3. Growing out of the previous section: give the singer something to sing. It may be enough to give the student the hint that Brahms used to judge a song by covering up everything but the words and voice part and the bass of the accompaniment. It is a good test. If the voice part is just following the dictates of the harmony of the accompaniment things are far from right.

4. Students are often unwise in their choice of words to set. Poetry of the very greatest kind rarely lends itself to musical setting. There is danger of gilding the lily. A solo setting of a Shakespeare Sonnet, or of a part of

Wordsworth's *Immortality Ode*, is hard to contemplate. Such things are complete in themselves. Poetry really suitable for music is of the kind which leaves something unsaid which music can say. Fortunately there is plenty of first-rate poetry which comes into this category.

Recitative and Arioso

In real recitative melody, accompaniment and set rhythm give way entirely to the words which assume almost complete ascendancy. At its best, however, the curve of the voice part will follow and illustrate the emotional content of the words, as also will the accompaniment, however slender. Recitative in its proper setting can be one of the most moving things in all music, as a short example from the *Matthew Passion* will show. It has obviously little or no place in the verse song, and must be used sparingly in the continuous setting type.

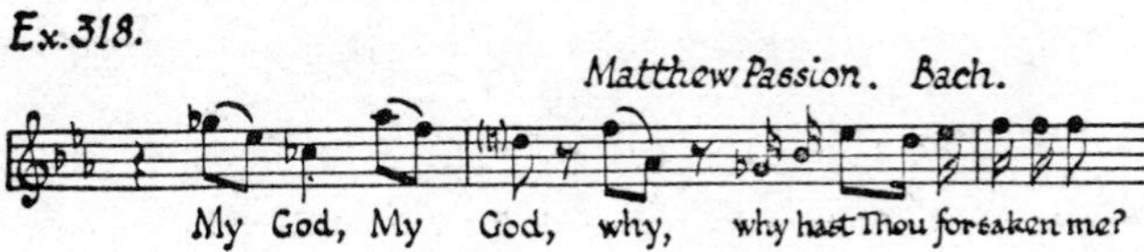

The modified forms, 'quasi recit.' and Arioso, are useful in extended settings, as contrasting sections or dramatic effects. One of the most beautiful examples which comes to mind immediately is the passage from Vaughan Williams's *Silent Noon*, a few bars of which are quoted:

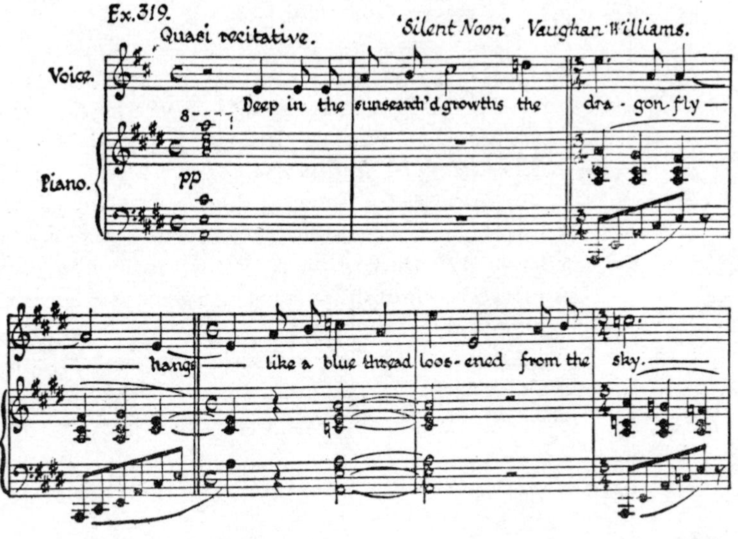

The whole of the second section of Schubert's *Death and the Maiden* is a 'quasi recit.'. His *Doppelgänger* is an even more striking example. It is one of the greatest songs ever written, and might be described as 'quasi recit.' throughout.

Chapter Eighteen

UNACCOMPANIED CHORAL WRITING

THE principles of setting words to music discussed in the last chapter apply to unaccompanied choral writing with slight modification. In simple, fairly homophonic writing for unaccompanied voices the highest part is generally the most prominent. It is therefore particularly necessary that its declamation of the words should be faultless. The lower parts in work not definitely contrapuntal cannot be expected to mirror the emotional rise and fall of the words by a responsive rise and fall of the melodic line; they may be regarded to some extent as an accompaniment. They must, however, have good verbal accentuation.

In definitely contrapuntal work each part ideally should mirror the words. The best work of the sixteenth and early seventeenth centuries, English and Italian, shows how superlatively this could be accomplished. The student should note how skilfully the composers of this period use homophonic passages alternating with contrapuntal work, each heightening the effect of the other.

One very important point must be kept in mind in contrapuntal work of this kind. The words are still of paramount importanee. They must be clear all the way through. Four voices each singing a different word or syllable at the same moment are apt to sound absurd. Unnecessary obscuring of the words in this way for mere contrapuntal effect is a common pitfall. Even some of the great English polyphonists were guilty of unfortunate jumbles of words.

Only by careful study and frequent hearing of polyphonic music (or even better by teaching it to a choir) can the student learn how to write clear vocal counterpoint. One of the best examples of clarity of words in (albeit fairly simple) counterpoint is Gibbons's setting of the evening Canticles in his *Short Service*. Another supreme example may be quoted:

In contrapuntal work the manufactured (verbal) accent > may be used freely, when the student knows his job, to obtain cross rhythms and independence of parts. Here again the English polyphonists are the supreme masters. The Byrd example quoted above is taken from a motet which contains some magnificent uses of cross rhythms and repays the closest study.

The melodic progression of the 'voices' must be carefully watched. The sixteenth-century rules regarding melodic intervals are even more important in unaccompanied choral writing than in vocal solos. Most polyphonic music in which these rules are kept presents no difficulty to a good choir as far as intonation is concerned. In much choral music from the time of John Sebastian Bach onwards instrumental melodic progressions (augmented and diminished intervals and large leaps) are used freely. Backed up by an instrumental accompaniment of sufficient weight this music is quite satisfactory in performance (though usually difficult and ungrateful to sing); but unaccompanied, the difficulties of intonation are well nigh insuperable. Another point is that unvocal and highly coloured chromatic intervals sound unsatisfactory even if sung correctly in tune according to our tempered scale.

Akin to this limitation is the difficulty of sudden shifting of the key centre to the more extreme keys, and the more difficult chromatic and enharmonic modulations. These, and most ambiguous and obscure chromatic chords, rarely sound satisfactory when sung (however well they may sound on the piano), a fact which is only too well known by choirmasters who have sensitive ears and are brave enough to tackle a good deal of the so-called choral music written by modern composers. The unsatisfactory sound of much modern choral music (especially unaccompanied) is not the fault (at least not always) of the singers. The plain fact is that the composer has usually misjudged his medium. Singers have to use their ears and imaginations as their only measure for pitching intervals. The ears and imaginations of most singers seem to be, by nature, not well attuned to the tempered scale in some of its modern uses.

All this does not mean that the student should become consciously archaic when writing for unaccompanied voices. What is required is that he should write music which will 'sing' well and achieve a really satisfactory effect in performance. Attention to the vocal line of each part—that is, making sure that it is grateful for the voice—will go a long way towards ensuring this.

Some technical points, with which the student is probably already familiar, may be worth recapitulating here.

A workable compass for the four types of voice usually employed is as follows:

Ex. 321.

One ghost from the nineteenth-century theoreticians may be laid. The fear of 'crossing the parts' in unaccompanied vocal writing still haunts many students. Palestrina, Byrd, and their contemporaries suffered from no such inhibitions. Their 'voices' move about through their particular compass with complete freedom and cross even parts not their immediate neighbours without hesitation or misgiving. In fact some of the most thrilling effects in unaccompanied singing are obtained by using the different registers of the voices with their characteristic 'colours' in the various combinations and permutations available.

Some further advice on 'lay-out' of the parts may perhaps be re-stated.

(a) Avoid a harmonic interval greater than an octave between an upper part and the part next to it in pitch. An exception is the interval between the bass (or, with reservations, lowest part) and the next upper part; this may be anything up to a tenth or even a twelfth.

(b) Except for special effects, it is better to avoid close intervals low down between the lower voices.

(c) Though actual crossing of parts is almost always good, overlapping is often clumsy, unless the overlap makes a consonant interval.

Ex. 322.

As in all good setting of words, the music must capture the atmosphere and at the same time be satisfactory from a musical point of view. Here again no one can teach a student how to do this. He must work out his own salvation, and his success will largely depend on the quality of his imagination and invention, his sensitiveness to words, and his artistic taste.

A few general suggestions may be of some help.

1. The form of any unaccompanied choral work will be dictated largely by the words. At the same time it must be musically satisfactory. The use of consistent thematic material, with judiciously planned contrasting sections, usually works well. As in the solo song, the 'verse' and the 'continuous' types somewhat modified, are available. In both types some kind of logical construction is essential.

2. Two of the most powerful means of expression in this kind of work

are: (a) the use of dissonance to underline some word or phrase of particular emotional significance (the less frequent the more effective). Akin to this is the melodic use of some unexpected interval.

(b) The use of a particular tessitura of the voices. For example, a high register to express joy, or tension (as in the Byrd example from *This Day Christ was borne*) or low registers to express the contrary emotions.

Ex. 323. *Peccantem me quotidie.* *Palestrina.*

3. A warning. Each voice, if it is provided with words at all, must have words that make sense when sung. Truncated sentences in the lower voices are all too commonly found, sometimes with considerable unconscious humour. Equally dangerous, and sometimes equally amusing is vain repetition of words and syllables. Some of Thomas Tomkins's work is spoilt by this.

The composer's reverence for the words he is setting should be sufficient guide. Sometimes a measure of truncation in the lower parts is unavoidable for musical reasons. See that what is left makes sense.

Vocalizing on 'oo' or 'ah' and humming with closed lips were much in fashion in the second decade of the present century. They can be very useful for purposes of accompaniment or special effect, and may possibly claim descent from some Tudor devices. They should be used with caution.

UNACCOMPANIED VOCAL FORMS

A few words must be said about some of the various types of unaccompanied vocal writing which form the literature of this branch of the art. (The liturgical forms need not be considered here.)

The Motet has a long and noble history from the dim ages of the thirteenth century to the present day. It is by origin a Latin church form. The first peak in its history came at the climax of the English and Italian polyphonic schools of the sixteenth century; the great motets of Byrd, Palestrina, Lassus, and many others are typical examples.

The chief characteristic of the motet as a musical form at this period is its highly developed contrapuntal texture sometimes interspersed with solid homophonic passages which greatly intensify the dramatic and musical effect. The words normally dictate the shape of the music, though in some cases a musical form independent of the words seems to be present. Examples of this are to be found especially in the English school. Byrd's advanced sense of musical structure has already been mentioned; Weelkes's fine motet, *Gloria in Excelsis*, has a definite ternary basis; in the Italian school a strongly felt musical design appears in such works as Palestrina's *O beata et gloriosa Trinitas*.

The second climax in the history of the motet is Bach's great set of works in the form. These works are designed on an almost symphonic scale with separate contrasted movements within the main structure. The contrapuntal texture still predominates, with more fully developed homophonic interludes sometimes extending to the length of a full movement. The use of chorale 'canti fermi' is a noticeable link with the old motet form (plain-song c.f.). Though these motets are complete as unaccompanied works it is probable that instrumental support (not an independent instrumental accompaniment) was given to them in Bach's time.

Later the term motet came to be used loosely to cover any important piece of incidental church music, accompanied or unaccompanied, and the essential character of the form was to some extent lost. True examples, however, continued to be written, such as S. Wesley's *Exultate*, and fine modern motets in English are represented by such works as Parry's *Songs of Farewell* and Vaughan Williams's *Prayer to the Father of Heaven*.

The essential qualities of the motet as known to-day remain much as they were in the sixteenth century, however different the language may be. They can be summed up as follows: (1) The motet is essentially a church work, designed for à cappella (unaccompanied) singing; (2) the texture is mainly contrapuntal with homophonic passages for relief or contrast; (3) the form is generally of the 'continuous setting' type as opposed to the verse-by-verse setting, often within a framework of some definite musical form.

The Madrigal in its true form may be regarded as the secular counterpart of the motet, though the contrapuntal predominance is less marked in it. As with the motet, a wide range of emotional feeling has been expressed in the form. The madrigal reached its highest point at the end of the sixteenth and beginning of the seventeenth centuries. In its most characteristic form it has largely dropped out of modern composition and has been replaced by the more direct 'part song' which will be touched upon later.

The Ballett, Ayre, Canzonet. These forms belong chiefly to the English madrigal school (though their counterparts can be found on the Continent). They are on the whole lighter, slenderer, and more homophonic than the madrigal proper. Their main technical difference is that they generally employ the verse-by-verse method of setting the words. The forms survive in practice in some types of modern part song.

The Glee was an eighteenth-century English product (*floruit* 1750–1830) properly for male voices unaccompanied. The form was a collection of mainly homophonic, short, self-contained movements. It has been completely superseded by the 'part song'.

The Part Song is a characteristically English form which evolved during the nineteenth century when the interest in choral singing was at its height. It is, as has been hinted above, to a large extent a compromise; several of the traditional unaccompanied vocal forms seem to have contributed to its generation. Like many mongrels it has proved to be a healthy specimen, and composers such as Parry, Stanford, and Elgar, have shown that it can be a vehicle for real musical expression ofia very high order.

The main characteristics of the form are: (1) it s written for an unaccompanied choir of either mixed or equal voices; (2) the texture is more often homophonic than contrapuntal, though part songs in which contrapuntal technique is used are quite often found; there is also a definite tendency to concentrate the main interest in the top part; (3) the verse-by-verse type of setting the words is most often found, though the continuous type of setting is equally possible.

There is a tendency among students when asked to write a part song to given words either to produce an elaborate pseudo-madrigal, or just an over-fed hymn tune. They have probably never realized that the part song, as a means of artistic expression, has quite a lot to be said for it. Its latent possibilities have been by no means fully explored yet.

In writing a part song it is just as necessary to use the medium of the unaccompanied chorus to its best advantage as in writing a string quartet. The individuality of the several voices should be treated with as much respect as that of the stringed instruments; each should contribute something vital to the whole.

It must not be forgotten that the aim of the part song is the musical interpretation of the words, just as in a solo song or any form of word setting. The value of any part song is its worth as music and as a setting of some particular words at the same time.

Some preliminary exercises on the subject will be found in the 'papers' at the end of the book.

Chapter Nineteen

THE HARMONIZATION OF BASSES (UNFIGURED), MELODIES IN ONE OF THE INNER VOICES, AND GROUND BASSES. WRITING FOR THE ORGAN

UNFIGURED BASSES

It must be taken for granted at this stage that the student can harmonize an unfigured bass with confidence and some artistry. Even so a few more or less elementary hints may be worth considering.

1. The harmonic rhythm of the bass must be realized. A given bass generally shows its harmonic changes and in fact all its harmonic implications more plainly than a melody. Accented passing notes and long and ornamentally resolved suspensions are the most common pitfalls for the inexperienced.

2. The task of writing a convincing melody over a given bass depends upon:

(a) realizing the harmonic rhythm and implications of the bass;
(b) finding the natural cadence points and phrase lengths;
(c) grasping the key scheme and modulations.

3. The texture of the music will depend entirely upon the character and medium of the given part. Here there is real scope for showing inventive and imaginative ability. The final test of a well-worked unfigured bass will be whether it sounds like a spontaneous piece of music, or merely so many 'parts' written above a given part. The hints which have been given in earlier chapters about working exercises in general, and special mediums in particular, hold good in dealing with basses.

4. A few technical suggestions may be added.

(a) A long bass note tied over the bar line (and, equally, a short one), and then descending by step, usually implies a suspension.

Ex. 324. (a)

(b)

It is also advisable to be on the look out for ornamental resolutions.

Ex. 325. (a)

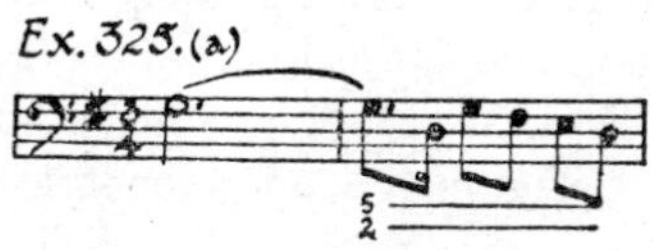

(b)

Repeated notes over the bar line, whether tied or not, nearly always demand a change of harmony. The anticipation on a preceding weak beat of a new harmony on the strong beat is usually bad.

(b) Accented passing notes and appoggiaturas must be recognized, and properly treated. When these are chromatic they are usually easy to recognize, but diatonic examples sometimes cause more difficulty. The student must rely on his harmonic sense.

Be careful not to quit an unessential note in the bass by leap. If such a position as the following should occur, it is clear, since the bass is given and cannot be altered (and provided that the setter of the question knew what he was doing), that the harmonic implication has not been properly realized. An accented passing ncte has usually been overlooked.

(c) In dealing with rests in a given bass part, it must be remembered that a rest on a weak beat does not cancel a preceding harmony.

(d) Beware of the $^6_4$ chord in harmonizing basses. The generally accepted rules governing its use, even if they seem pedantic, are worth following if the chord is used at all. It may be observed that the given bass part may become at times a 'middle' or even top part, and by this means many bad $^6_4$s can be avoided.

MELODIES IN ONE OF THE INNER VOICES

These should present few difficulties, and there is really nothing to add to what has already been said about harmonization of melodies in general, except to stress the vital importance of sketching in the bass first of all. The treatment of the exercises will then depend merely upon the style of the given part.

GROUND BASSES

The ground bass might well have a book to itself. It is a most important form of composition which has attracted composers from the thirteenth century (*Sumer is icumen in*) to the present day (Walton: *Henry V*, incidental music; Britten: *Peter Grimes*).

Whether it is a subject really fit for the student to tackle is open to question; but as it crops up frequently in examinations, and is incidentally a very useful technical study, it must be included here.

The ground usually consists of a short and simple phrase, normally (but not necessarily) in the bass, repeated a number of times with varied treatment. The superstructure may take the form of (a) a more or less consistent and continuous melodic line, simply accompanied, over the repeated bass, or (b) an elaborate set of variations upon the ground.

An examination of some specimens of grounds will show what can be done with the form. A very early example may be seen in the famous 'Reading Rota' (*Sumer is icumen in*). Here the ground appears in canon, while the four upper parts say their say, also in canon. It belongs to (a) type. The following material should enable the student to reconstruct it:

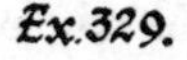

Grounds.

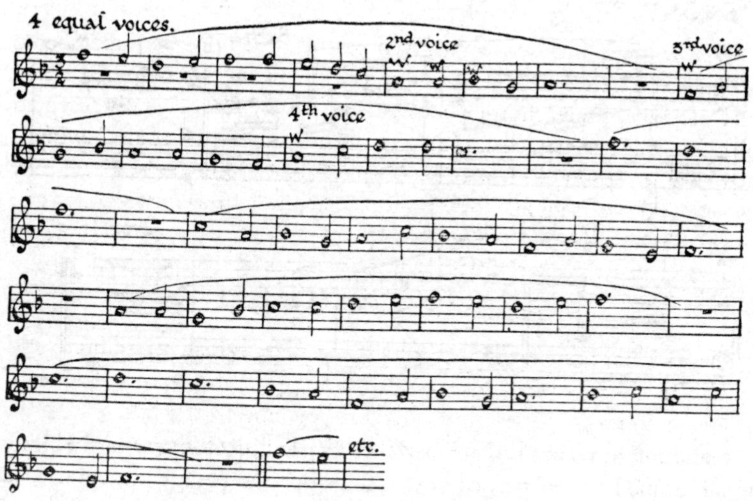

The treatment of the Purcell period is well seen in *Dido's Lament* and the famous *Evening Hymn on a Ground*. The former is a good example of independent melodic writing over a ground, type (a); the latter combines the melodic line idea with variations.

Of the full-fledged variation form, type (b), Bach's great organ *Passacaglia in C Minor* is a supreme example. The structure of this tremendous movement deserves the closest study. The grouping of the variations, the contrasts, and magnificent series of climaxes, make it one of the great things in music.

The ground in full orchestral panoply can be seen in the last movement of Brahms's E minor symphony, where it can be traced in harmonic outline, even if not always in exact thematic appearance, right up to the coda. The student has much to learn from Brahms's masterly handling of this closely knit variation form. These are just a few examples out of many which will repay detailed examination.

Some consideration must now be given to the technical problems of the variation type of ground. Much has been written about the necessity for avoiding full closes at the end of each repetition of the ground, yet in Bach's great organ example all the variations except two end with a definite full close (V–I), (those two are merely Vb–I and 7Vc–Ib) and no feeling of monotony or scrappiness results. The fact is that the whole thing depends on how the cadences are handled. Bach avoids coming to too many halts by the continuity of his counterpoint. The melodic line often runs on over the cadence, or a new figure begins on the cadence. Brahms does the same.

The thing to realize is that a perfect cadence does not necessarily imply a halt. Some halts are needed, just as full stops and paragraphs are needed in writing English; the music can, however, go on building up or releasing emotional tension despite V–I progressions, and it is only the repetition of unwanted halts that disturbs the continuity of the movement. The avoidance of the full close has its uses. Its danger is that it often sounds forced and unconvincing. Rheinberger has some good examples of its effective use.

To sum up: avoid halts, except when necessary as marking the end of a paragraph, by continuity of a melodic phrase over the cadence, by beginning a new figure on or before the cadence, or more sparingly, and only if it sounds completely convincing, by avoiding the perfect cadence harmonically.

With regard to the harmonic scheme and modulations the usual advice given to students is to analyse the ground thoroughly, and note all possible harmonizations and modulations. This is a good move if the student is prepared to discard all the possibilities which sound in the least forced, however ingenious they may be.

The following example will give some idea of the possibilities in this line, and what to discard:

This is, of course, only a harmonic sketch, showing some possible alternative harmonizations. Section 1 shows perfectly obvious simple harmonization. Section 2 some reasonable alternatives, with a modulation to C major. In Section 3 the harmonization at A is rather weak, and unless useful for figure development, is not worth including. The augmented sixth at B might be useful with its implication of E major (or minor). The modulation at C to F major avoiding the perfect cadence is somewhat clumsy and though it might be worked in, it would probably never sound completely convincing. In Section 4 the inversion of the augmented sixth at D sounds forced and is probably better ruled out of court. The progressions in the remainder of this section (E onwards) are definitely forced and it would require very judicious handling to make them sound natural. The seventh at F is weak and had better be discarded. In the fifth section the D minor modulation is probably useful.

This short investigation does not exhaust the harmonic possibilities of the ground, but it probably gives enough scope for ten or twelve variations.

The variations will group themselves into two main categories: (a) melodic and harmonic interest, ranging from a simple melodic line accompanied by straightforward harmony, to complicated treatment of arpeggio figures on the harmonic basis of the ground: (b) contrapuntal treatment, including possibly independent canon and imitative writing over (or below or around) the given ground, or some part in canon with the ground itself.

The ground is by no means always kept in the lowest part. In the Bach organ example it appears in middle or upper parts (Variations 11, 12 and 13). In the Brahms example cited it appears all over the orchestra. Nor need it always appear in its original form. Bach uses a shadow form in Variations 14 and 15 of the organ *Passacaglia*, and ornamented and broken up statements in Variations 5, 9 and 13. Brahms, using his theme freely in upper parts, pushes these devices even further.

The use of 'pedals' should not be overlooked. When the ground is in an upper part a pedal anchorage in the bass is sometimes a welcome change from a constantly moving bass part. Inverted pedals can also be used. The ornamented inverted pedal at the end of the Bach example is a thrilling climax (see Example 341).

The shape of the work as a whole, whether it be of six repetitions of the ground or of twenty-six, must be carefully planned. No chance arrangement of variations, however good they may be individually, will ever prove to be really satisfying. The things to aim at are: (a) groups of variations growing out of each other, even in short examples, rather than individual and isolated variations; (b) one or more climaxes; (c) contrast, generally of one group of variations with another, rather than between individual variations.

WRITING FOR ORGAN

As most ground basses are set for organ, a few paragraphs must be added on writing for that instrument.

The manual compass is (on average instruments) from to 8ve. The pedal compass from to or . These notes sound in pitch as written if 8-ft. stops are used; if a 16-ft. stop is drawn the sound produced is an octave below the written note (normally 16 and 8-ft. stops are used together on the pedals, giving an octave bass) a 4-ft. stop sounds an octave above, and so forth.

The manual technique is much the same as in the case of the piano, but two important differences must be borne in mind. The organ does not boast of a 'sustaining pedal'. A note goes on sounding just as long and only as long as the key is held down; so some care is necessary on the part of pianists writing for organ, else they may misjudge the effect.

Ex. 333.

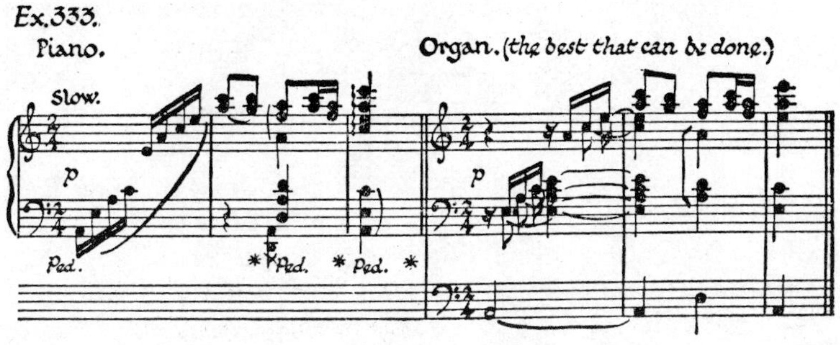

The second difference is that a note sounded remains of the same intensity till it is released, unless the stops are changed (or the swell box opened or shut). This makes nuances difficult on the organ, especially from the more subtle accentual aspect—although a good deal can be done by phrasing, semi-staccato playing, and judicious use of swell pedals. It also removes chances of glossing over certain notes in a chord, and making others more prominent (modernists beware). This defect is to some extent reduced by the helpful provision of two, three, or four manuals, with a variety of stops of different power and colour on each. The student should get some organist friend to initiate him into the mysteries of this much abused instrument, which, whatever superior people say about its clumsiness, is in reality at its best a magnificent means of musical expression, for which some of the finest music in existence has been written.

A final word about the pedals. A good player can do most things that a normal bass part is likely to demand, but it is well to remember that long scale passages at quick speeds or extended arpeggios are ineffective and difficult. The best way to learn how to write for the organ in general and the pedals in particular is by a close study of Bach's organ works.

Basses for harmonization.
1. for String Quartet.
Lento.
'Cello.
p
mf
f
p
f
p
pp
2. for String Trio or Quartet.
Allegro.
'Cello
f
dim
p
cresc.
f
3. String Quintet.
Lento.
'Cello
p
p espressivo
f
p
pp
4. String Quartet.
Allegro molto.
'Cello.
f
cres.
ff
mf
f
pizz.

Ground Basses.
Henry Purcell.
1 Andante.
2 Andante.
3 Andante moderato.
4 Andante.
5 Lento.
6 Allegretto.
7 Andante.
8 Allegro.
9 Moderato.
10 Andante con moto.
11 Allegro.

Chapter Twenty

PEDALS

A PEDAL is a note sustained generally, but not invariably, in the lowest part, while the other parts move, either in consonance with the held note or forming new harmonics themselves.

The older theorists only recognized pedals on the tonic and dominant degrees of the scale, and refused to countenance modulation during a pedal. In actual practice the notes of the scale which may be used as pedals are in no way restricted, nor is modulation.

More importance must be attached to the text-book rules about starting and quitting pedal points. The rules insist that at the beginning of a pedal all parts must make good harmony with the note to be sustained; on the point of quitting the pedal this same condition must apply, and the progression from the last chord of the pedal to the next chord must also be correct. A special word of warning must be given against quitting a pedal incorrectly on a $\frac{6}{4}$ chord.

Double and even multiple pedals are available; in fact a whole chord may in certain circumstances be used as a pedal. Decorated pedals are frequently found.

In sixteenth-century church music pedals and inverted pedals (sustained notes in some upper part) are freely used, generally at the end of a movement. Some examples will show the typical process:

The English madrigalists made great use of the device, as often in the middle of a movement as at the end. Many daring and highly successful experiments appear in their work. Dr. Fellowes in his *English Madrigal Composers* quotes some most interesting examples, among them a moving passage from the second part of Weelkes's *O care, thou wilt despatch me*, where a bit of delightfully naïve but very effective word painting is done; the words are 'but thou dost now sustain me' and the music, on a dominant pedal runs as follows:

By the time of Bach and Handel pedals had become a fully developed part of technique. Bach made constant use of them, often with tremendous effect. The opening of the F major organ toccata is a fine example of a long canon over a tonic pedal. The first five bars of the opening chorus of the *Matthew Passion* may well be quoted to show his freedom in using implied modulation over a pedal point.

An even more striking example comes from the end of the third 'Kyrie' from the *Clavierübung*, Book 3. The pedal begins on a $\frac{6}{4}$ which resolves normally.

A good case of a pedal in an inner voice comes from the end of the fugue on 'Jesus Christus unser Heiland' (*Clavierübung*, Book 3):

The last two variations in the organ *Passacaglia* show a fine use of an inverted and decorated double pedal in the upper parts.

The Mozart–Haydn period shows little change in the use of pedals, which occur frequently and tend to become formal, on the lines of this Haydn example:

Occasionally much more striking use is made of inverted pedals; the following example from Mozart's D minor quartet is most moving.

With Beethoven the treatment of pedals assumed a much more intense significance; the more or less formal use of the Mozart–Haydn period was replaced by a new forcefulness and emotional power. The following illustration, a double pedal (tonic and dominant) shows the dramatic possibilities.

Ex. 344. Symphony V. Beethoven.

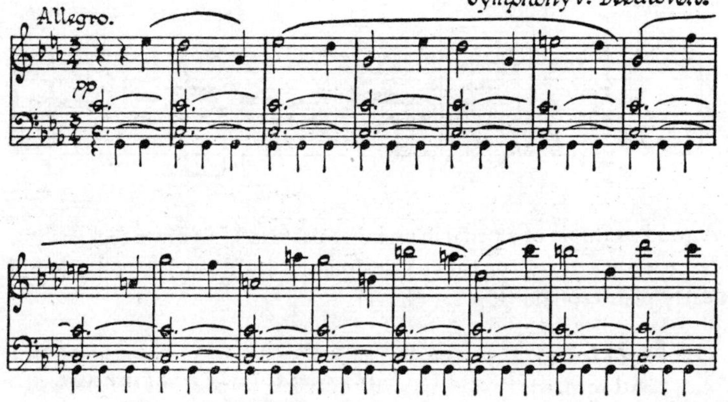

Allegro.
pp
cresc.
ff

Beethoven did not suffer from the theorist's inhibitions about quitting a pedal 'correctly', as the example below (quoted by Prout) demonstrates.

Ex. 345. Op. 14. No. 2. Beethoven.

Andante.

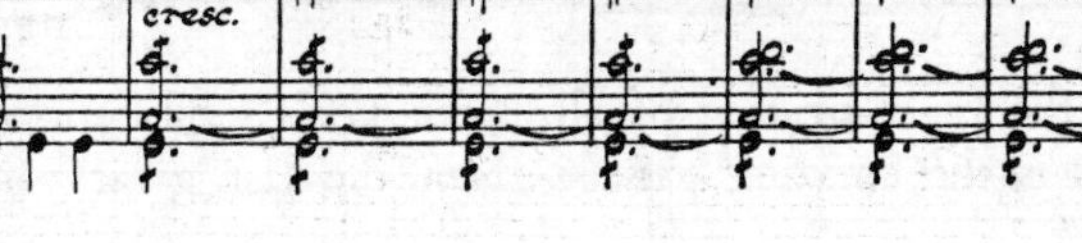

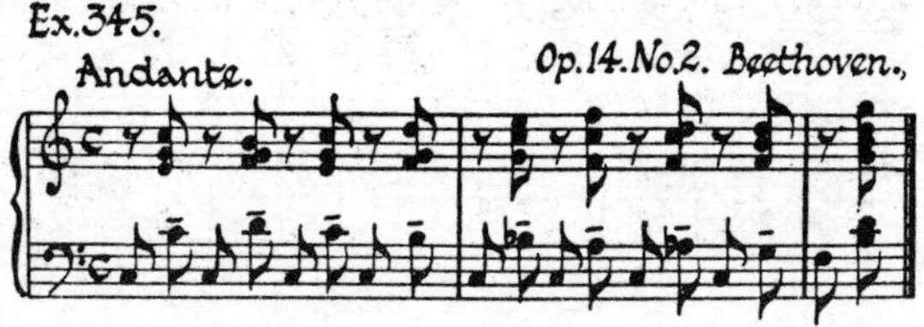

The treatment of inverted pedals in Beethoven is even more emancipated. In the example from the slow movement of the fifth symphony the E♭ pedal in the top part on the clarinet remains through a transition to B♭ minor, and then, with complete disregard for text-book propriety, but fine effect, moves up a semitone to an E♮.

A good example of a pedal in an inner part clashing quite recklessly with notes a second away on either side (quoted by Prout) is to be found in an early piano sonata (Op 27, No. 1).

Perhaps the most striking of all Beethoven's explorations of pedal possibilities is the amazing passage from the last great piano sonata

(Op. 111). The key at the beginning of the passage is C major (the C♯ being an appoggiatura) so this is apparently an example of an inverted pedal on the supertonic. During the pedal a very definite modulation to E♭ is made; the pedal note is therefore quitted as the leading note of the new key. It may also be noticed that Beethoven has no more hesitation about starting a pedal on a dissonance than about his unconventional ways of quitting one.

It is not necessary to give a detailed survey of the use of pedals since Beethoven; the subject is vast, since the device has proved to be one of the most useful parts of technique of musical composition. A few additional examples of general interest must suffice.

Ex. 351
"Götterdämmerung." Wagner.
Hagen.
Alberich.
tr

Ex. 352.
Pedal on the subdominant. (7th of Dominant Harmony.)
Tschaikowsky.
Moderato
3
Tempo I°.

Ex.353.
Decorated pedal.
Allegro moderato.
2nd Symphony Sibelius.
Timp.(#)
tr
3
3
etc.

Chapter Twenty-One

EXERCISES

As this book is intended to be of use to students of musical theory, it has been thought wise to include a set of 'Papers' roughly on the lines of the Harmony Papers set in some universities. As much variety as possible has been included in the type of question set, and an honest endeavour has been made to make the questions interesting and musical.

I

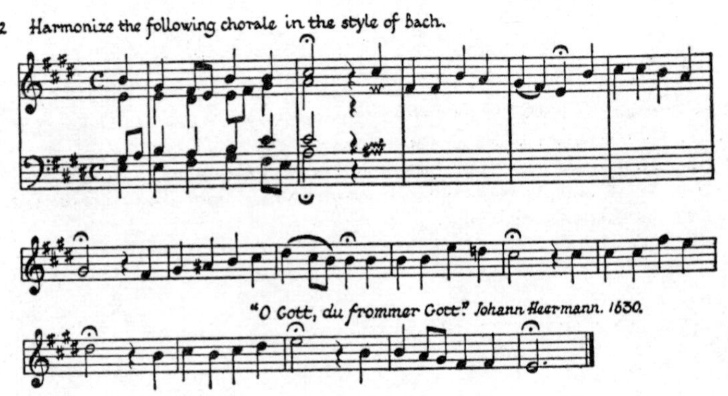

EXERCISES

II

1 Add parts for S.A.T. to this bass of a chorale in the style of Bach.

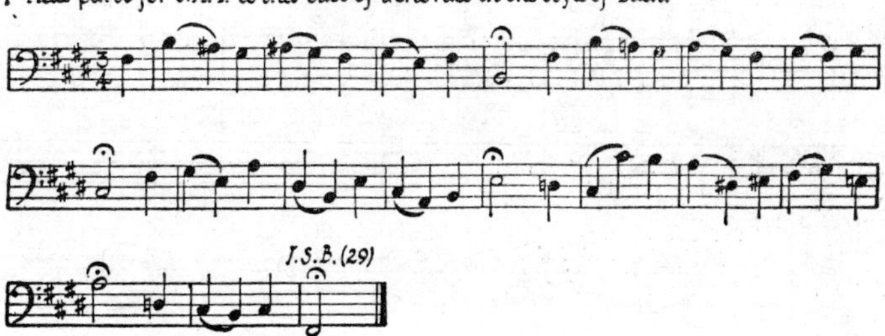

2 Complete the following string trio.

3. Harmonize this melodic fragment for four voices.

(a) In A minor: using plain diatonic harmony without modulation.

(b) In A minor: using some chromatic chords without modulation.

(c) In C major: using diatonic and chromatic harmony and touching D minor in bar 2.

(d) Without restrictions.

EXERCISES

III

EXERCISES

IV

1. Complete the following pianoforte accompaniment.

IV (continued)

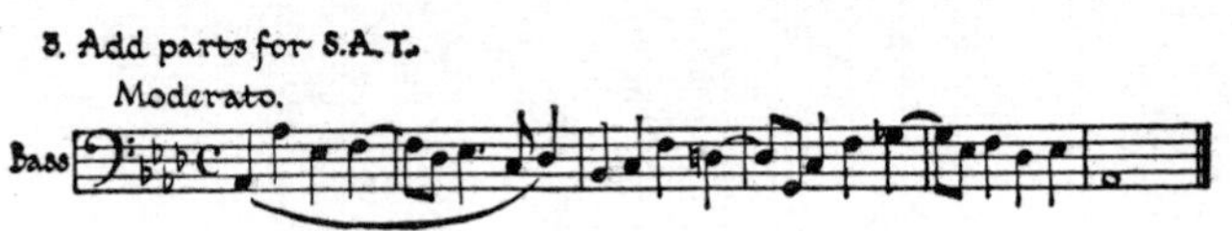

EXERCISES

V

1. Add parts for Vn. I, Vn. II, and Viola to the given 'Cello part: the suggested opening may be used.
Moderato.
Vn I
Vn II
Viola
'Cello
mf
f
mp
ff
pizz.
arco p
pp
2. Complete this partsong fragment (S.A.T.B.)
O Love! they wrong thee much That say thy sweet is bitter When thy rich
fruit is such As no-thing — can be swee - - ter. Fair — house of joy and bliss,
Where truest plea-sure is, I do a - - dore thee I know thee what thou art, I
serve thee with my heart — and fall — be - fore thee.

EXERCISES

VI

1. Complete the following string quartet. (Use open score.)

2. Write a short scherzo for piano in simple Binary or Ternary form on the given opening.

EXERCISES

VII

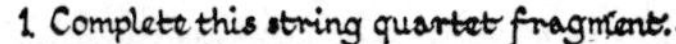

2. Explore the harmonic possibilities of the following ground bass – 4 or 5 versions (some of them possibly interlinked) should be shown. The harmony may be indicated by plain chords, though an outline of the top part or any useful 'figures' may be given. The whole should represent first stage preliminary work for writing a short passacaglia.

3. Add parts for Soprano, Alto and Bass to this tune by Orlando Gibbons. (Tenor)

VIII

1. Add a piano accompaniment to this oboe part: the given opening may be used.

2. Harmonize the following melody in the style of a Bach chorale. Use passing notes freely. (S.A.T.B.)

IX

1. Complete this part song for S.A.T.B.

2. Write a short Scherzo for string trio on this opening.

EXERCISES

X

Regard this fragment for string quartet as a 'theme for variations'. Write (1) a variation beginning as suggested at (A) leading to (2) a scherzando variation in a major key in some compound time. (3) A variation as suggested at (B) leading to (4) a short coda.

2. Add parts for S. S. A. T. above this chorale Bass.

(276. O Ewigkeit, du Donnerwort.) J. S. B.

XI

1. Harmonize this hymn tune in simple four part harmony – (S.A.T.B. unaccompanied.)

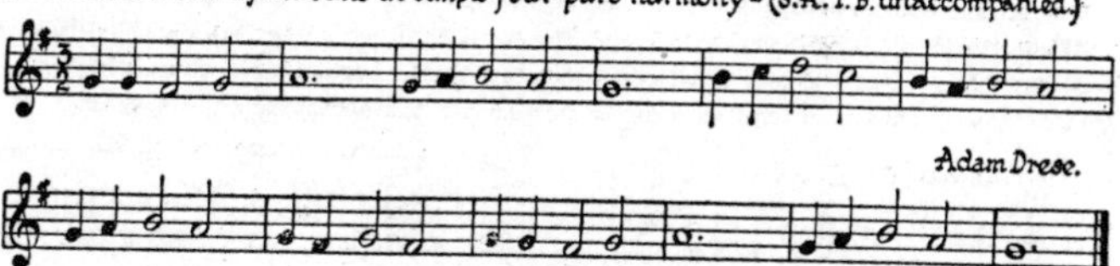

Then, (a) Write a free organ accompaniment for the above hymn tune beginning as follows:

(b) a descant verse with the tune in the tenor. (S.A.T.B. unaccompanied)

Use the following words in this verse. The ending should be extended so as to form a short coda:

Blessed, heavenly light,
Shining through earth's night;
Voice, that oft of love hast told me;
Arms, so strong to clasp and hold me;
Thou thy watch wilt keep,
Saviour, o'er my sleep.

(c) Bind the three versions together into a whole by supplying a short organ introduction with interludes between the verses. The organ may join the voices in the coda.

EXERCISES

XII

The 'theme' given below, for clarinet and string quartet is intended for variations. Complete the first four variations from the suggested beginnings given; then write a fifth variation leading to a final variation and coda. Breaks may be made between the variations or they may lead into each other at the discretion of the student.

EXERCISES

XIII

1. Complete the following as a duet for violin and viola. The technical resources of the viola should be freely used.

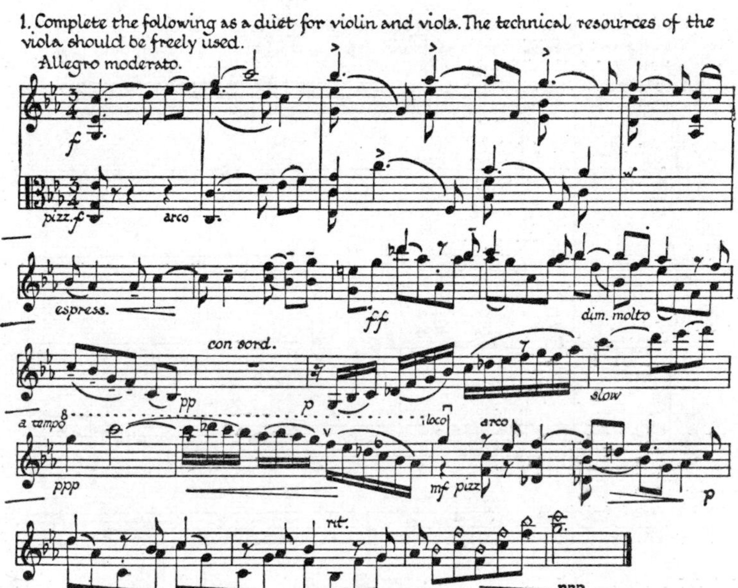

2. Write a short passacaglia for organ on this ground. (5 or 6 variations plus coda.)

EXERCISES

XIV

1. Complete this Bach chorale arrangement for 3 (high) trumpets,  chorus: S.A.T.B. and continuo. The trumpets and continuo should be used for the interludes.

Martin Luther 1535.

2. Write a short passacaglia for string sextet (2 vns. 2 violas, 2 'celli) on the following ground.

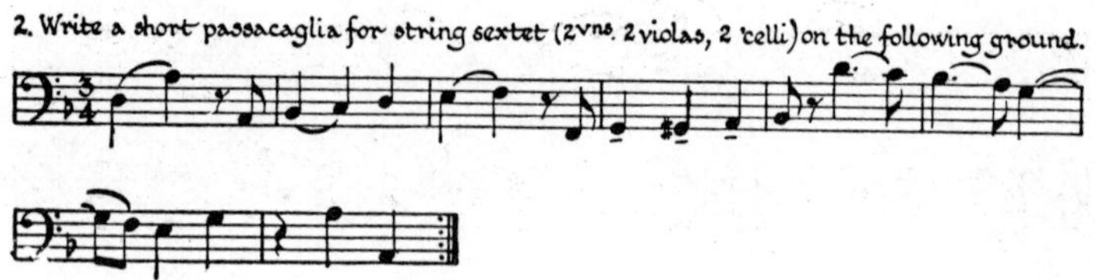

EXERCISES

XV

1. Complete this Bach chorale arrangement for 4 part chorus and three trumpets in C. (7 parts) The compass of the trumpets may be regarded as from [music] to [music]. They should be kept in fairly close position.

2. To the following part for first viola, add parts for Violin I, Violin II, Viola II, and 'Cello. The first phrase may be treated as a solo, and used by the other instruments later.